Young Writers

Spellbound

Essex

Poetry Now
Young Writers

Edited by Dave Thomas

1998

To G'ma & G'pa

A signed copy for when I'm rich and famous!
Lots of love

Anna Batson
x x x

First published in Great Britain in 1998 by
POETRY NOW YOUNG WRITERS
1-2 Wainman Road, Woodston,
Peterborough, PE2 7BU
Telephone (01733) 230748

HB ISBN 1 86188 863 5
SB ISBN 1 86188 868 6

FOREWORD

In this, our 5th competition year, we are proud to present *Spellbound Essex.* This anthology represents the very best endeavours of the children from this region.

The standard of entries was high, which made the task of editing a difficult one, but nonetheless enjoyable. The variety of subject matter, creativity and imagination never ceases to amaze and is indeed an inspiration to us all.

This year's competition attracted the highest entry ever - over 46,000 from all over the UK, and for the first time included entries from English speaking children living abroad.

Congratulations to all the writers published in *Spellbound Essex.* We hope you enjoy reading the poems and that your success will inspire you to continue writing in the future.

CONTENTS

Gregory Isaacs 1
Bradley Jacob 2

Beal High School

Fozia Islam 3
Litticia Lawlor 3
Katherine Wong 4
Jonathan Hart 5
Gurleen Kathuria 6
Samantha Frankel 7
Zenam Khan 8
Amanda Bassett 9
Jeannine Syalon 10
Oliver Yaros 11
Paul King 12
Rashmi Kalra 12
Mobina Maqsood 13
Nazia Farookhi 14
Claire Snewin 15
Rehman Soobhan 16

Beauchamps Grant Maintained School

Hayley Trott 16
Morgan Nash 17
Lorna Fleming 17
Rachel Wilson 18
Cheryl Agius 18
Andrew Craig 19
Tom Galbally 20
Katie Antill 20
Kerry Fulcher 21
David Fisk 22
Adam Buttwell 22
Adam Davis 23
Katie Winter 24
Clare Strong 25

Ben Robbins	26
Stephanie Pace	26
Joanne Severn	27
Richard Shelley	28
Sam Moss	28
Emily Browne	29
Kim Rayner	29
Rebecca McCutcheon	30
Matthew Draper	30
Julie Neaves	31
Peter Battersby	32
Debbie Williams	32
Maria Sullivan	33
Helen Medland	33
Lori North	34
Liane Pitcher	34
Sarah Beecher	34
Mark Pitchford	35
Hannah Ferguson	35
Katie Luther & Kerry Hughes	36

Chelmer Valley High School

Natalie Nunez	36
Joanne Piddington	37
Jamie Godden	37
Matthew Jarrett	38
Carly Mann	38
Richard Jarrett	39
Holly Henry	40
Richard Morgan	40
Katie Faramarzi	41
Hannah Miller	42

Finchingfield Primary School

Cassie Harvey-Smith	42

Frances Bardsley School for Girls

Victoria Davies	43

Victoria Loomes	43
Jennifer Bull	44
Natalie Thomas	44
Abida Siddiqi	45
Jade Stoner	45
Sarah Ann Rutland	46
Nina Wallace	46
Leanne Bryan	47

Gable Hall Secondary School

Adrienne McCormack	47
Lisa Gardner	48
Kirsty Beard	48
Louise Ockendon	49
Laura Fenneberg	50
Helen Gillan	50
Danielle Ireland	51
Adam Russell	52
Sam McQuade	53
Stuart Mobsby	54
Barry Page	54
Maria Holland	55
Leanne Archer	56
Naomi Wilson	56
Lee Wightwick	57
Mikaela Wakefield	57
Jamie Percival	58
Matthew Guscott	58
Laura Randall	59
Louise Graves	60
Dean Maguire	60
Kimberley Portas	61
Lara Sutherland	61
Michael Westley	62
Jodie Harrison	62
George McAllister	62

Havering VIth Form College

Robert Linham	63
Sarah Pym	64
Maria Tyler	65
Lucy Brace	66
Melanie Wilkins	66
Matthew Hart	67
Colin Budge	67
Anna Kristine	68
Louise Fairweather	69
Sarah Gonputh	70
Rachael Eastwood	70
Katherine Challis	71
Kelly Chesterton	72
Joanna Warwick	73

Ilford Ursuline High School

Porsha Roache-Robinson	74
Meera Kataria	74
Bobby Chowdhury	75
Camilla Bhachu	76
Nishani Balendra	77
Eleanor Kirby	78

King Harold Grant Maintained School

Victoria Jackson	78
Danielle Cox	79
Tony Seary	79
Toni Brown	80
Joanne McPeake	80
Victoria Ravenhill	81
Claire Newman	81
Martin Burr	82
Andrea Cave	82
John Hall	83
Luke Power	84
Jade Fitzjohn	84
Adam McInerney	85

Emma Ward	85
Christopher Gough	86
Kayleigh Westall	86
Nicola Smith	87
James Schroder	88
Nina Maffei	88
Hazel Stelzner	89
Latoya Johnson	90
Jennifer Davis	91
Rachel Boulton	91
Joanna Farley	92
Tiffany Harold	92
Georgina Brant	93
Lucy Bridges	94
Lisa Flaxton	94
Josh Knights	95
David Hoye	95
Maria Savill	96
Adam Taylor	96
Lisa Cashman	97
Shelley Webb	97
Gemma Lowe	98
Chris Martin	98
Olivia Dunne	99
Sally Pritchard	99
Sadie Stares	100
Daniel Coghill	100
Robert Elliott	101
Emily Gapes	101
Lisa Gubbings	102
Charlotte Thompson	102
Paul Jackson	103
Tim Hempsted	103
Edward Stelzner	103
Nicola Bull	104
Lorraine Keogh	104
Pamela Sideras	105
Dean Godtschalk	105

Miyase Dogan	106
David Fisher	106
Sarah King	107
Clare Simper	107
Paul Clarke	108
Kirsty Conlon	108
Samantha Ball	109

Marshalls Park School

Chris Valentine	109

Rainsford High School

Hollie Kemp	110
Sarah Allison	110
Anna Bateson	111
Michelle Levene	112
Carla Wise	113

St John's C of E School

Shona Hales	114
Rachel McCue	114
Rosalind McGuire	115
Jennifer Cordell	116
Karen Hurley	117

St Nicholas School

Kunal Patel	118
Victoria Marnoch	118
Simon Black	119
Emma Goodfellow	119
Bradley Exall	120
Zahra Paliwala	120
Gregory Crabb	121
Hayley Matthews	122
Andrew Cherrill	122
Hannah Barry	123
Jessica Atkins	124
Archchana Radhakrishnan	125

Lauren Harris	126
Katie Furlong	126
Carlene Banister	127
Sarah Naylor	128
Natalie Polaine	129
David Brierley	130
Bobby Ghadami	131
Emilie Bedford	132

Shoeburyness County High School

Amy Webb	132
Jodie Abraham	133
Christine Adams	134
Nicola Wood	134
Sarah Haines	135
Gemma McNevin	136
Vickie Dann	137
Jenny Wilson	138
Lena Drew	138
Sophie O'Donoghue	139
Matthew Leggett	139
Tom Hatley	140
Elisha Ross	140
Ross Ellis	141
Anthony Davis	141
Wayne Carter	142
Claire Paine	143
Andrew Turner	144
Charlotte Reading	145
Melanie Jerrum	145
Glyn Parsons	146
Aaron Osborn	146
Crystal Warrington	147
Liam Shaw	148
Jonathan Watson	148
Richard Choules	149
Anna Tansley	150
Dawn Callowhill	150

Joe Clements	151
Adam Shuttleworth	152
Adam Salmons	152
Emma Sheehan	153
Kylie Jenkins	154
Anthony Crinks	154
Daniel Rivers	155
Claire Parish	156
Michele Davies	156
Vicki Wells	157
Jenny Crouch	158
Alex Cuthbert	158
Donna Horner	159
Tommy Dickinson	160
Mark Jarvis	160
Susan Pleasant	161
Charlotte Smyth	162
Joanne White	162
Laura Cornwell	163
Louise Thomas & Laura Watkins	163
Stephen Craven	164
Rupert Chappell	164
Michael Box	165
Amy Varney & Jodie Treveil	166
Rupal Kataria	166
Laura Needham	167
Samantha Bromfield	168
Caroline Burwood	168
Jessica Stackhouse	169
Beth Spreadborough	169
Tracey Whitbread	170
Stuart Norris	171
Natalie Munro	172
Helen Barnecutt	172
Ben Sandford	173
James Jones	173
Grant Bailey	174
Gregory Crowhurst	174

Claire Allen	175
Julie Smith	176
Matthew Wells	176
Jenny Haysom	177
Chris Stanford	178
Henrietta Ross	178
Linzi Tegerdine	179
Natasha Monerville	180
Adam Mack	180
Tina Wagstaff	181
Rebecca Acklam	181
Samantha Treveil	182
Sam Dawson	182
Ruth Wareham	183
Donna Rennell	183
Amanda Wilkinson	184
Adrian Woolner	184
Amy Barns	185
Alison Lindsay	185
Kerry Malone	186
Lynette Rees	186
Kate Day	187
Sarah Hulbert	187
Rohee Khalique	188
Amy Sullivan	189
Charlotte Dersley	190
Michelle De-Pass	190
Mark Delf	191
Katherine Ball	192
Kelly Bowers	192
Emma Tansley	193
Kelly Wall	194
Daniella Tullio	195
Vicky Whitehair	195
Timothy Ballantine	196
David Bonsall	196
Chloe Haddow	197
Rachel Rose	197

Thomas Penasa	198
Michelle Kinsalla	198
Wayne Morris	199
Nick Brooker	199
Matthew Overall	200
Natasha Morris	200
Charmaine Breakwell	201
Ashley Mills	202
Katie Brown & Jemma Jarvis	202
Natasha Reed	203
Nicola Snelling	203
Ryan Bollu	204
Daniel Rapley	204
Carla Boydell	205
Wayne Reed	205
Roy Thompson	206
Jody Purbrick	206
Lee Cody	207
Daniel Allen	208
Kevin Rushman	209
Emma Harper	210
Nicola Cook	210
Iain McCann	211
Laura Sage	212
Stacey Healy	212
Scott Harrington	213
Louise Jowett	214
Nina May	214
David Cartwright	215
Sarah Goodfellow	215
Danny Smith	216
Natasha Allen	216
Chai-Wai Chung	217
Jamie Brown	218
Alex Blyth	218
Charlotte Coster	219
Mark Pearce	220
Claire Bassett	220

Ella Donoghue	221
Trevor Hixon	222
Gemma Doodes	222
Samantha Rudd	223
Jodie Page	224
Gemma Milner	224
Stacey Petty-Mayor	225
Leanne Newman	226
Danielle Chelton	227
Christopher Bysouth	228
Steven Church	229
Lauren Moore	230
Peter Radmall	230
Kayleigh Hooper	231
Joanne Pearl	232
Linzi Carrington	232
Robin Gray	233
Joanne Jowett	234
Adam Gardner	234
Kelly Lander	235
Katie Bishop	235
Hollie Driscoll	236
Nicholas Riches	236
Adam March	237
Lisa Merrin	237
Warren Franklin	238
James Dixon	238
Anna Woods	239
Charlotte Ford	239
Thomas Squires	240
Lisa Cousins	241
Kate Martin	242
Suzie Solly	243

The Appleton School

Charlotte Davis	243
Angela Faux & Kirsty Paterson	244
Jenna Furby	245

Samantha Fellows	245
Hayley Smith	246
Faye Neate, Jo Eggleston, Taryn Diamond & Jane Foley	246
Chloe Farrugia	247
Emma Reed	248
Heather Turner	249
Matthew Guenigault	250
David Broad	250
Sophie Lockwood	251
Donna Greene	252
Marie King	253
Jo Shuttlewood	254

The Billericay School

Ashleigh Drake	254
Jennifer Hard	255
Jemma Perry	256
Martin Horn	257
Ruth Fallen	258
Amy Marshall	259
Alex Dorney	260
Katie Wakefield	260
Zoie Snazell	261
Hannah Warren	261
William Crighton	262
Robert Neale	262
David Green	263
Joseph Bird	264
Luke Holloway	265
Nina Gibbons	266
Joanne Oakman	267
Laura Cowell	268
Gemma Brown	269
Claire Scoot	269
Heather Willis	270
Benjamin Chapman	270
Debbie Harlow	271

Sheree French 272
Tony Cox 272
Jonathan Wong 273
Jodie Selfe 274
Phillip Gilbert 275
Karla Sears 276
Laura Walker 276
Ian Yates 277
Adele Lamb 278
Claire Bedford 278
Robert Kerr 279
Nicole Strayer 280
Alison Perry 281
Nicholas Butler 282
Victoria Jackson 282
Michael Deats 283
Ellie Childs 284
Sarah Flatman 285z
Antony Harvey 286
Mari-Clare Speller 287
Katie Jenkins 287
Todd Row 288
Catherine Cowell 289
Kelly Kendall 290

The Fitzwimarc School

Stephanie Gilbert 291
Mark Warren 291
Jenna Kirby 292
Michael Thomas 293
Andrew Chapman 294

The Greensward School

Tom Pickering 294
Emma Ashpole 295
Melanie Rogers 295
Emma Kirby 296
Sarah Toomey 296

Kylie Thompson 297
Hannah Frost 298
Emma Souster 298
Naomi Bessey 299
Rebecca De-Koning 300
Claire Cross 300
Laura Wilks 301
Charlotte Frankis 301
Ross Gregory 302
Emma Barnard 302
Kerry Waters 302

The King John School

Carol Greenland 303
Keith Smith 304
Sarah Maddex 305
Joanne Webb 306
Holly Carder 306
Jo Palmby 307
Matthew Gardiner 308

The Notley High School

Vanessa Long 308
Anthony Overy 309
David McLernon 310

The Plume School

Stuart Morley 311
Kate Pratt 312
Alun Causaker 313
Helen Tarling 314
Katharine Youle 314
Hannah Nobbs 315
Claire Vincent 316
John Randall 316
Jo Messenger 317
Matthew White 318
Jamie Lauder 318

Denise Long	319
Lisa Gardiner	320
Sadie Bell	320
Emma Clarke	321
Louise Wheeler	322
Mark Wallis	322
Susie Barnfather	323
Kelly Hancox	323
Karen Farrell	324
Rachel Finch	324
Kelly Ramsden	325
David Wallis	326
Claire Edwards	326
Katie McCambridge	327
James Boutle	328
Claire Sharp	329
Zoë Allen	330
Natalie Hodge	330
Melanie Newman	331
Vickie Cumbers	332
Emma Newman	332
Gemma Boreham	333
Charlotte Hodge	333
Charlotte Corderoy	334
Vicky Pegram	334
Thomas Ellum	335
Samantha Clarke	336
Karen Anderton	336
Debbie Mansell	337
Sophie Parmenter	338
Louise Etherton	339
Nicola Lunn	339
Sarah Pithers	340
Alys Twinley	340
Helen Hill	341
Gemma Everitt	341
Louise Woolnough	341
Emma Bolton	342

Charlotte Mack	342
Tim Collins	343
Kate Leney	344
Jason Scadding	344
Oliver Whyman	344
Rachel Staines	345
Kerry Mackenzie	345
Lynette Hurley	346
Andrew Renwick	346
Stacie McCabe	347
Laura Moseley	347
Tania Musolino	348
Lee Schofield	348
Hayley Yates	349
Andrew Wright	349
Matthew Hailstone	350

Valentines High School

Karen Rose Tumbridge	350
Aisha Ali	351
Laveeza Zafar	351
Claire Hamilton	352
Mahwish Iftikhar	352
Lucy Geraghty	353
Westley Parasram	353
Ria McIntosh-Henry	354
Benjamin Clarke	354
Scott Lester	355
Nadine Chatergon	355
M Ahsan Ali	356
Leanne White	356
Asmaa Nadat	357
Aadila Ahmed	357
Sarah Everitt	358
Nicholas Illman	358
Gemma Butler	359
Hafsa Pasta	360
Simon Waxkirsh	360

Farzana Patel 361
Sheraz Razaq 361
Shama Hussain 362
Reena Bhudia 362

Wanstead High School
Jor'el C N Mitchell 363
Christopher Waldron 364
Karla Williams 364
Gareshma Bhatia 365
Carly Zucker 366
Sharon Payne 366
Amy Ward 367
Omar Ahmed 368
Hatice Boza & Sophia Rehman 368
Rowan Wheeler 369
Harriet Sinclair 369
Natalie Fehily 370
Louise Panteli 370
Laura Davies 371
Sean James 372

William De Ferrers School
Jamie Hoare 372
Philip Hart 373
Vicki Swallow 373
Oliver Swainson 374
Alex Westbrook 374
Adam Boorman 375
Kate Hollingsbee 375
Adam Biggs 376
Rachel Wright 377
Helena Gretton 378
Laura Gardner 378
Ian Newman 378

THE POEMS

Trapped In A Dream

Dreams can be mysterious, scary or funny,
Dreams can be cheerful, happy and sunny,
But *beware!*
Dreams can't always be fair,
When in the land of a dream,
You could be trapped, it may seem

You enter a dream unexpectedly,
Then you're stranded, you don't have a key,
This is a dream when you know where you are,
It seems like reality is so far,
In this dream you can have fun,
But when bad appears just *run!*

You're running away,
'I'm going to get you' it will say,
It suddenly hits you,
You finally know what to do,
Realising you're in a dream,
You turn around and from your finger out shoots a laser beam,

The thing blows up,
You've won the Bedtime Cup,
You punch and hit,
There's the exit,
I'm lying in a duvet sea,
Hey! What's that trophy!

Gregory Isaacs (12)

ALWAYS THERE

This life is teeming with false starts,
With broken dreams and broken hearts.
But there's a way that we can win,
By thriving on the strength within.

An open mind can always see,
The path to take, the destiny.
A willing heart will always guide.
The flame within, the hope inside.

The road ahead seems so unclear,
But love can catch your every tear.
Though all the good cards have been laid,
The faith is strong, will never fade.

There's always someone loving you,
To face the bad, and get you through.
Although sometimes it's hard to cope,
There's love,
There's me,
There's you,
There's hope.

Bradley Jacob (17)

Trapped

The hard abrasive power of the cold, damp floor,
Rubbed against her feet like nails on a board,
The dull grey walls surrounded her in pain,
And the cobwebs in the corner sent a shiver down her spine,
She walked towards the door,
She felt as if she was walking through an ocean of fears,
She looked at the ceiling and felt the walls cave in,
Now she could feel it,
Her lungs filled with dusty smoke,
And her heart nearly stopped,
She couldn't move,
She couldn't breathe,
But there she was,
Stuck in a box,
All alone with nothing but memories of her sadness and fear.

Fozia Islam (16)
Beal High School

Poem For Diana Princess Of Wales

A heart of gold stopped beating,
two smiling eyes at rest,
God broke our hearts
to prove to us he only takes the best.

Although I didn't meet you and now I wish I did,
Although you're up in heaven in my heart you'll always live.

So many broken hearts around the world,
and one of them is mine,
But as you'd say,
be strong, be wise and remember special times.

Litticia Lawlor (12)
Beal High School

RUSSIAN GYPSY

She was Russian.
Wandered the streets.
Her eyes,
Ice blue sapphires,
that glittered in the light.
But at nightfall.
Sunken like the sunset,
Drowned into the velvet night
like her eyes, changed a violet mist
Hair like woven silken melting to
liquid in the
blackness.
Her porcelain skin like a doll's so
sharp against the night
Lips the colour of
scarlet
blood.
An almost cat-like
grace,
When she danced.
Pure elegance.
Figure frail and
fragile.
When she looked
up the stars
twinkled like jewels
When she smiled
the world lit up.

Something, something about
her.
Indescribable
I don't know her name
I don't think she had
one.

Katherine Wong (12)
Beal High School

ONE WINDY DAY

(In loving memory of Aunty Lily, who sadly passed away on Saturday 10 May 1997)

You always sat by the window
For months on end you'd sit
A flickering flame about to go out
Whose cinders can't be re-lit.

So you became embittered
Like a harsh wind on a summer's day
Tossing and turning and rocking the boat
Hoping you'd never sail away

They told you things would get better
But they didn't say
That a hand from the heavens would sweep you up
On a windy day

Now you're with the angels
Cleaning up the sky
Polishing the windows
For others to sit by.

Jonathan Hart (17)
Beal High School

My Love

My life has no meaning
A dark shadow it seems,
No light but darkness
Shines upon me.
I'll wait for you, till the end of time
Not knowing what's on your mind,
Loving me or hating me,
It's driving me crazy
I think about you all the time.

I wish you happiness
And everything you desire
Your smile so sweet,
Your eyes so deep
Showing the love and warmth you may have for me.
Illusions I see
Including you and me
Will I ever get you
Impossible it seems.

I'd do anything for you
One chance is all I ask
Loving you will be my only task.
People will come and people will go
But my love for you will never die
And one thing I know
I love you so much
I can't explain why.

Gurleen Kathuria (16)
Beal High School

Sea Of Thoughts

A field of dreams, destinies and hopes
Stars and seas contain the secrets,
the truths and depths of thoughts,
The power of hearts.
The blue tones tumble down,
reflecting the dark and mysterious sides,
Trying to work out the feelings and darkness of the mysterious world.
The frustration and misery fade and happiness is released.
The fragments of minds and imaginations are brought to life
opened and expanded in depth, detail, but most of all reality.
Freedom is not put aside,
and thoughts escape while the deep darkness plunges down.
Deeper and deeper to the depths of the seas.
The mysteries surface and the happiness shoots up,
taking over and working its way *to the top,*
up to reach and join the stars.
The sea stirs and the stars twinkle.
Their attention is powerful and affection is shown,
to those who gather and admire their beauty.
Whilst brainwashed thoughts are gathered
and the seas get stronger, more powerful and clever.
the stars get brighter and are influenced to show.
Rivers, lakes and streams are formed
Along with light, dreams and fantasies.
Thoughts are carried, drifted and float
Whilst others stay and maybe cope with the reality and sense of
a glowing mind,
dreams are lost and twisted in time.

Samantha Frankel (15)
Beal High School

NOT A LIFE WORTH LIVING

Trapped by the many walls of her destiny,
Desperate for love, suffocated by duty.
Forced against her will, against her whole being.
All for their all encompassing greed,
Greed for power, and for money.

Someone else's property soon,
Decided the day she was born.
Like a chattel, to be bartered, when of age
For money in exchange for her life,
To be cornered for eternity in a loveless marriage.

Frantic as a fox caught in a trap,
Wanting to break free; not enough strength for it.
Barely controlled, a panic wildness in her eyes.
Her life turned over into the hands of a tyrant.

A manic gleam in his rolling eyes,
Hinting at his streak of violence.
His rotten, yellow teeth leering in anticipation.
She knew he wanted to tame and kill her soul,
He the hunter, she the hunted.

Her life an almost unrealistic tragedy.
Not worth living she thinks.
A calmness, emanating from her skin,
As the welcome decision is made.

Just a visit to the medicine cabinet,
And all would be well.
Truly not a life worth living, she thinks,
As she drifts into sweet oblivion.

Zenam Khan (16)
Beal High School

THE DOLPHIN

The dolphin the most
intelligent mammal.
Dives into the water as
smoothly as can be.
As it starts to swim up
to the surface.
The crystal clear water
shines from the sun
on its skin and it looks
at me. As it dives round
deeper, deep, deep.
I can see the dolphin's
eye have a quick and little
Peep!

He swims around in a
circle but his eyes are
still set on me.
His eye twinkles in the
sun. I was thinking,
if he was in a race
I bet he would have
won. If you put a dolphin
to a test
He would win there's
no doubt about it.
The dolphin is the
Best!

Amanda Bassett (12)
Beal High School

The Lights And Shadows Of Nature

For the first time in my life, I am encountering hidden pathways,
That were once sheltered by a canopy of overlocking trees.
I am being lead through cylindrical tunnels,
That have been created by desolate, striving animals,
And I am following a narrow stream,
That has no rivers or seas to merge into.

I never imagined, in my wildest dreams,
That these discreet places ever existed.
Until the day when all the clouds,
Rapidly swept over me in unison,
And instantly revealed, into my world,
Was a sphere of blazing light.

The shining sun,
Streamed through my previously sealed windows,
Glistening over the contents,
Until they shone with clarity and precision.
The gleaming rays emphasised,
The greenness of a single leaf, the delicate feature of each tiny animal,
And the richness in the blue, of the sparkling stream.

But the inspirational brightness of the light,
Must have an equilibrium of darkness to accompany it.
That causes the trees to be destroyed,
That endangers the animals and creates for them fear,
And pollutes the streams, so they are no longer clear.

The purpose of this, is to prevent us from seeing,
The end of the path, the tunnel or stream.
And until this day,
I will never know when the sun will shine a bright light,
Or never know when a cloud will cast a shadow.
All I know is that to destine the fate of the good and the bad,
Nature must be able to take complete control,
And in order for it to succeed, I must follow my soul.

Jeannine Syalon (17)
Beal High School

HOSTAGE

Plunged into darkness, that's what it's like,
Led down many stairs and doors before light is seen again,
In a 12 x 12 foot room you'll spend the rest of your days,
Sitting, standing, walking, eating,
Sleeping, reading and reflecting.
The cries and shouts of inmates are all you can hear, grovelling for salvation,
And for those long since departed.
If you dare to listen, your mind will undoubtedly be thrown down,
Deep down into the chasm of madness and indifference.

Forgotten by the world, you spend the rest of your time, alone with your mind,
Exploring the unreachable, touching the untouchable.
Longing for the day when you reach for freedom, and escape.
For many, the bell will toll for them in this place,
But for others it offers the promise of salvation and hope.

Oliver Yaros (15)
Beal High School

WHEN SATURDAY COMES

When Saturday comes,
the anticipation of what may be.
After a week of sadness,
the nation's grief condensed into a prolonged silence.

The silence perfectly observed,
a fitting tribute to England's Rose.
As a candle glows,
the whistle blows.

Gascoigne, Wright and Scholes with the goals,
the sadness and sorrow turn into smiles,
a wonderful performance for a wonderful lady.
Only days after England's Rose was peacefully laid to rest,
the England lads did it for their Princess.

Paul King (15)
Beal High School

ALONE

How does it feel to be alone?
To not be loved;
to spend each day searching, hoping,
of what might be or what is.

Wandering through the lush meadows, deep in thought.
An emptiness nothing lying ahead.
Not a hope of a dream, a future looking bleak.

Someday the light will shine,
the path, will be shown.
Until that day,
carry on searching, hoping . . .

Rashmi Kalra (15)
Beal High School

To Love Him So Much . . .

Acting, so I don't want them to know,
Letting my love go by
Like an unwanted show.
Why is this happening only one can know,
Not even a touch but, I have to love him so much.

It disappeared like the stars,
Came back like the sun,
It hurts like the most painful pain,
It feels like your emotions are going up in a plane.
Time is needed to cure the hurt,
Was time predictable of birth?
What am I talking of? Only I can know,
Not even a touch but, I have to love him so much . . .

I thought it had gone,
But it was still there,
Deep inside me, handled with care.
Desperation is one thing,
This is not that,
Although I let it walk over me, like I am a mat,
Under the feet of a wild cat.
Not even a touch but, I have to love him so much . . .

A glossy image and a few thoughts remain,
But I still want to gain.
A glance will place happiness in my act,
But that will remain that.
Not even a touch, but what led me
To love him so much . . .?

Mobina Maqsood (16)
Beal High School

THE STATE OF LOST LOVE

The one I loved did not care
The one I loved did not share

I felt so sad
And I felt so alone
Although I knew
my love could never have known

The light inside my soul was so dim
And every morning
or whenever he would walk in,
I would feel myself begin to shine
Yet I knew
deep down inside
My true love would never be mine

Now he is gone
I'm still on my own
Trying to grasp inside of myself
The yet unknown

The one I loved will never care
The one I loved will now never share

Nazia Farookhi (15)
Beal High School

Princess Diana, Queen Of Hearts

A Princess to our nation,
A hope to all in need,
A light in all the darkness,
A perfect person to lead.
A mother to your children,
A beautiful shining star,
A lighthouse off a rocky shore
Warning boats not to go too far.
A hearing for the deaf,
A sight for all the blind,
A shoulder for all to cry on,
An image of all that's kind.
Diana we'll always miss you,
You will never be replaced,
And forever in the world's heart
A void that can't be replaced.

Claire Snewin (15)
Beal High School

DIANA

Diana was the queen of hearts,
She was always on the top of my charts,
Her beauty and compassion was the best
She definitely passed the test.

She reminds me of my friend Meriline,
Diana was my heroine,
She is the greatest woman I have ever seen,
Diana was a woman that was very keen,
But the media kept her curled,

Diana lived her life in the media,
And was sometimes in the encyclopaedia,
Her popularity grew worldwide,
Now we blame the paparazzi for her death,
And the drunk driver for making her life end so quickly.

Rehman Soobhan (11)
Beal High School

MANCHESTER UNITED

Manchester United is the name of the team,
Football is the game.
It is the best, has always been,
Will always be the same.
Giggs, Beckham and the Nevilles too
Scholes, Butt and Keane.
They are brilliant, I'm telling you
Strange as it may seem,
To have a girl talking about football,
It's not just a boy's thing!

Hayley Trott (13)
Beauchamps Grant Maintained School

DREAMS

Thinking, standing,
Faces, but no names.
Like a cow to slaughter
Alone.
The stage alight with thunderous applause.
A sense of well-being fills the air.
It's my life, my way, my all.
A feeling that can't be matched.
I tell myself.
Shivering, help, help me please!
A mouth opens - no words come out.
A trigger is pulled in my brain
Speaking is easy
All fear has gone.
The cheers erupt from this heavenly place
My dream is fulfilled
I wake up
Just a dream.

Morgan Nash (16)
Beauchamps Grant Maintained School

IT'S LOVE

My feelings I devote to you,
Can only be described as love.
I don't know what you think of me
Perhaps I'm just another young girl,
But whoever I am to you
You will always be my love.

Lorna Fleming (13)
Beauchamps Grant Maintained School

SPELLBOUND

I am the sunlight shining down for
all to see,
I am the sky long and clear for all
to be free,
I am the love inside growing into a
sweet caress,
I am everything which is real, everything you
can touch,
I am the ground you walk on, I am not
too much
I feel spellbound - overwhelmed with my
dreams
I am my own, smile glowing as it gleams.

Rachel Wilson (15)
Beauchamps Grant Maintained School

FALLING AWAY

Flying through endless sheets of the night sky,
Floating above rivers wild, watching life go by.
Feeling like a lost feather in a morning breeze
Falling to the melody of the singing trees.
Up above the clouds to an existence unknown
To the open gates friendly faces are shown.
Saying my final goodbye to people who were near
Peacefully falling asleep there's nothing more to fear.
In this pearly heavenly land
Peaceful tranquil sound
Death is such a strong word
I'm purely sleeping - spellbound.

Cheryl Agius (15)
Beauchamps Grant Maintained School

At Dead Of Night

At dead of night in bed I sleep,
Through a thousand visions drifting deep,

Deep within my spellbound mind,
To my inner recesses where I find:

A world of awe, and timeless mystery,
Of magic, deceit, war and myth.

Of creatures vast, wild and free,
A world which belongs to me.

Where magician Merlin chants his awesome powers,
And unicorns roam, play and eat the flowers.

Where witches cackle, and pilot their brooms,
During the evening when darkness looms.

A world where mermaids rule the seas,
And giant spiders spin webs in trees.

A world where ogres, trolls and goblins battle
For lands vast and far,

A real fighting fantasy!

And every night I visit this place,
Surviving the horrors which I face.

And every morning I am found,
Lying strewn on the floor - Spellbound!

Andrew Craig (16)
Beauchamps Grant Maintained School

Snake Catcher

Feel like a snake catcher ready to pounce
Catching and killing snakes by the ounce.

Striding through the long green grass
Carefully putting on my mask.

I see one, I want, I get one
It weighs no less than a ton.

I catch it, I kill it, I shred it
I sell the skin and take the credit.

I know it's cruel, but I just don't care
I need all the money to pay for my fare.

Like a snake catcher ready to pounce
Catching, killing, selling snake skin by the ounce.

Tom Galbally (14)
Beauchamps Grant Maintained School

Spinning

I lie on the floor and close my eyes,
I'm lost with only fear inside.
My head spinning like a fairground ride,
And I think to myself the reason why.
Why do I do the things I do?
Is it so I can be like you?
Or is it just because I'm scared?
Of the memories of people who cared.
I need to talk to someone,
But I wouldn't know where to start.
How do you tell somebody
That your world's just fallen apart?

Katie Antill (15)
Beauchamps Grant Maintained School

GRANDAD

Losing someone you love,
just like losing a friend
standing at the window-pane
watching the rain,
hearing the thunder.
Thinking about the lover
He lost, the friends he left
relatives crying, mourning
some people just thinking.
Maybe it was fate
Why does God take the
special ones?
Just out of the blue.
I sleep that night and
think of the times we had
together and the things we did.
I wish I had seen him before
He passed, to tell him that
I loved him.
Just one last time.
I hope he is watching me mourn
for him.
I just sit there crying just in
a world of my own.

Kerry Fulcher (14)
Beauchamps Grant Maintained School

HEART OF DARKNESS

All through the night I feel a dark and twisted power.
As the seconds tick by, each one passing like an hour.

My mind is filled with the pain of regret,
Lying on my bed in a raging sweat.

I dream a dream about my life,
Living in anger depression and strife.
Why do I bother? Day after day
You walk straight by,
Should I ask you to stay?

I feel the darkness calling me back
I run in fear on an endless track.

With or without you,
Time goes by,
We live our lives and then we die.

Pain fills my heart and anger rages through,
My darkest nightmare is a life without you . . .

David Fisk (16)
Beauchamps Grant Maintained School

STEAM DAYS

Clickety clack, clickety clack,
goes the train over the track,
through the tunnel and over the bridge,
past the station by the hedge.

Into the valley full of trees,
across the river, steam into the breeze,
slipping sliding along the rail,
travelling through rain and hail.

It starts to get darker, the sun's going down.
Houses flash by now, approaching the town.
A stop at the station, people get off.
The day's almost over, the crew's had enough.

Faster and faster the steamer goes,
until a hill approaches and all becomes slow.
With the driver exhausted and the fire nearly dead,
the engine returns for a rest in the shed.

Adam Buttwell (13)
Beauchamps Grant Maintained School

AIRPORTS

Airports are busy
They can make you dizzy
Tax free, or duty free
It doesn't matter to me
There are people boarding planes
And people boarding trains
Someone coming
Someone going
Someone waiting
Someone sleeping
Someone parking
Someone annoying
In your way
After you have been delayed
At last you get to the other end
This foreign place drives you round the bend
But I do like to fly a lot
Because I'm the pilot.

Adam Davis (13)
Beauchamps Grant Maintained School

WEIRD INSANITY

I've been having one of those days,
you know!
Where you wake up in the morning,
and your face has sprouted a squillion spots.
Or when you're standing waiting for your friends
who are always late
then it starts to rain.
Your hair's stuck to the sides of your head,
your make-up's rolling down your face,
down your body,
and lands in a puddle in front of your feet.
Is this just me in a daydream,
Spellbound to the reality of this life?
Is it really sunny and bright outside
of my twisted mind?
Or is the reality of my life
about to jump out and smack me in the face?
I am spellbound,
Spellbound in my own imagination
of weird and wonderful thoughts.
Can I escape from this?
Free me from this world of weird insanity.

Katie Winter (15)
Beauchamps Grant Maintained School

Birds

I wish I had wings,
I think I might
fly by day,
rest by night.

A bird,
can fly about all day,
over rooftops,
miles away.

Soaring high and flying low,
looking out for friend and foe.

Springtime is busy,
making nests for the young.
Summer comes quickly,
hot days have begun.

Autumn berries are easily found.
In winter, food is scarce upon the ground.

In winter I think I'll stay,
tucked up tight,
safe from the cold,
on snowy nights.

Clare Strong (14)
Beauchamps Grant Maintained School

Private Detective

Through the shadows the detective creeps
The ground he walks and the lights he leaps
His long brown coat wraps round him like a snake
And his camera, pictures it will take

In his office he rests his feet
A woman walks in and both their eyes meet
She sits on his desk and gives him a task
Then the detective puts on his mask

Bad guys he will fight
Steering wheels on cars he'll hold tight
Women he will save
And take them through a booby trapped cave.

At the end of the day
He can truly say
'I saved the world as we know it'

As he walks through the crowd and wipes his feet on a mat
A little old lady runs up and shouts
'Thanks for saving my cat.'

Ben Robbins (13)
Beauchamps Grant Maintained School

Friendship

A shoulder to cry on.
Someone who's there.
That's all you need,
Somebody to care.

A chat on the phone,
A really good cry.
That's what you need
They're there to help you by.

Secrets shared
And promises made
A friend is always there
No need to be afraid

A shoulder to cry on.
Someone who's there.
That's all you need,
Somebody to care.

Stephanie Pace (13)
Beauchamps Grant Maintained School

My Hamster

A small, round fur ball
Sandy, white with black eyes
And little pink ears.

His name is Ronan,
He's very cute and cuddly,
When I hold him tight.

He has long, sharp teeth,
Which wouldn't hurt a soul,
He is very tame.

He's trapped in a cage,
He wishes he could be free,
So I let him out.

When I leave the room,
Eyes begging for me to stay,
But still I leave him.

Joanne Severn (13)
Beauchamps Grant Maintained School

ALIEN DOGS

Their heads are really big,
but their bodies are long and thin.
They really love to dig
and their brains are rather dim.

They bounce around all day
Chasing currant buns
they hide them in the hay
and eat them when they're done.

The doggies' eyes are bulging
Their noses alert for smells
Their tentacles start rolling
when ding goes the dinner bell.

Richard Shelley (13)
Beauchamps Grant Maintained School

PRISONERS OF WAR

Sharpen your spears,
We are coming,
Nowhere to hide,
The war is at your door,
We are coming.
The cattle and the young have fled,
Just the old and weak to fight,
Sharpen your spears,
Because tomorrow we will come to Soweto,
We are coming.

Sam Moss (14)
Beauchamps Grant Maintained School

My Dog

A golden ball, all huddled together,
A sad looking creature,
with no life ahead.
No attempt to get up,
not a shudder or a shiver,
lying there lifeless, a golden lump of fur.

His black beady eyes,
begging for pity.
His big pointy ears,
all drooped and saggy,
and his long wet nose,
which makes him look unhappy.

He can't get up, or run, or play.
He eats and sleeps without a moan all day
He looks at me with a tear in his eye,
I wish I could help my lifeless dog.

Emily Browne (13)
Beauchamps Grant Maintained School

The Water

The water laid peacefully and still,
It trickled slowly down,
Flowing in and out the hills,
Curving and wriggling from side to side,
Leaves would fall in happily,
To them it was like a water slide,
The water gushing about and around,
Took its chance pushing itself off a rock
Falling smack! On the ground.

Kim Rayner (14)
Beauchamps Grant Maintained School

Forever Over

I'm drowning in seas of frenzied flashing
And I've gone to something I don't understand
Unaware if anyone cares, or if there's anyone there
I'm dead to the world until I come in to land
Just spinning, in the lucid waves of convulsions
Crazy to fight to stay where I want to belong
Holding on, when it's impossible to grip
Refusing to succumb to the world that's an eternal storm
Nobody will accept what's happening to me
But I know it's real, like the planets and the stars
Wish I wasn't here, lost in the danger
So very near, and yet so very far
So scarred by something no one cares to mention
Plagued by something no one dares to say
And my memories are gone whenever I take a trip there
I even forget I do not want to stay
A place I've only revisited in my nightmares
But I can tell it's going to haunt forever over.

Rebecca McCutcheon (13)
Beauchamps Grant Maintained School

Nirvana

There is a large city that belongs in the sky,
Where all of the children learn to fly.
All of the people are happy there,
For all of the thoughts are light and fair.

The gates are of pearl
And the streets are like gold,
Faces full of colour and life.
Their lives are peachy, their bellies are brimmed
And the people forget their once troubled strife.

And standing on top, above His people
'There is the Saviour,' they sing
'There forever and there for all,
Keeping us under His wing.'

There is a large city that belongs in the sky,
Where all of the children learn to fly.
All of the people are happy there,
For all of the thoughts are light and fair.

Matthew Draper (15)
Beauchamps Grant Maintained School

ALONE

My life is like a hell-hole,
Burning in the ground,
I have no friends, no family,
There's just no one around,
I wonder what it would be like,
To have someone that cared?
To tuck you in,
Kiss you goodnight,
To help you say your prayers.
It's no good dreaming,
My dream will never come,
I have to face the fact,
That I am the only one.

Julie Neaves (15)
Beauchamps Grant Maintained School

My Grandad

It's seven years ago today
Seems like it was yesterday
Even though I was young
My life will never be as much fun
I never thought the day would come
When a life would disappear behind the sun
It may seem silly after seven years
But thinking of him almost brings me to tears
He was like a shining star to me
He was never trapped but always free
I only knew him as my Grandad who will never end
But when he died I knew I'd also lost my very bestest friend.
I love you Grandad wherever you are

Peter Battersby (14)
Beauchamps Grant Maintained School

Spellbound

*S*un's down, full moon's up,
*P*otions and spells,
*E*nhanced by the abrupt.
*L*ittle old ladies in big black hats,
*L*ittle creatures known as black cats.
*B*roomsticks and cauldrons
*O*r black magic spells,
*U*ndo the puzzles of a living hell.
*N*obody messes with a little old witch,
*D*eath or despair, you can be bewitched.

Debbie Williams (15)
Beauchamps Grant Maintained School

FAMILIES

Families can be started,
Families can be stopped,
Families can be separated,
Then families cry a lot.

Children get upset,
Children often cry,
Children want to stay,
But Daddy goes away.

Daddy misses Mummy
Mummy misses Daddy
The children miss them both so much,
They wish they'd kept in touch.

Maria Sullivan (13)
Beauchamps Grant Maintained School

THE WIND

The wind rustles through the trees
Sometimes just a little breeze,
But hurricanes rip houses apart
Toss them up, that's just the start
Cars and trains are thrown around
Flying animals pulled from the ground
The waves from the sea crash
The hurricane enjoys the splash
At last it's over, out comes the sun
The children all party, it's such fun.

Helen Medland (13)
Beauchamps Grant Maintained School

Lonely

All alone in the cold night air,
No family or friends no one to care,
Unhappy and cold feels so alone,
Sits on the beach just watching the sea
As the moon shines on the glistening water
And the wind blows the calming waves,
for a second she forgets her loneliness,
Then she remembers all over again.

Lori North (13)
Beauchamps Grant Maintained School

Loneliness

Rejection once again,
What's wrong with being more than friends?
Is it me, the way I act
I know it's a well-known fact
That I'm not the most popular in
My school and get laughed at in
The dinner hall.

Liane Pitcher (14)
Beauchamps Grant Maintained School

The Secret Garden

The smell of the flowers
and the smell of the trees,
unlocked by a secret key.

The sound of the birds
and the sound of the trees waving,
unlocked by a secret key.

The sound of children
and the sound of the waterfall,
unlocked by a secret key.

Sarah Beecher (14)
Beauchamps Grant Maintained School

My View

I gaze out of the window,
Hills and trees were to my left,
Spoilt by the gigantic hideous pylons,
Vaguely spread about,
To my right is the town,
Leaden and cheerless,
With graffiti on the stockades,
And I contemplate the morning dew.

Mark Pitchford (13)
Beauchamps Grant Maintained School

Poem

My ideas fill the page in my mind,
But they are useless.
The words fill my head,
But they mean nothing.
The rhythms tap a beat,
But they are noteless.
The trail of lines and phrases,
Already have been used.
Why does writing poems,
Make me feel confused?

Hannah Ferguson (13)
Beauchamps Grant Maintained School

School's Out

As the bell rings,
We push in our chairs
The door goes bang, as we run down the stairs,
There's a rush for the vendors,
The money slots in,
A rustle of papers,
Then we head for the bin.
I speed to the gate as crowds await
So much for rushing, Charlotte's late.

Katie Luther & Kerry Hughes (13)
Beauchamps Grant Maintained School

Seasons

Four seasons, the scenery is changing, turning like a wheel,
A season comes, another goes as the sun sets over the hill.

In winter the snow falls gently to the ground
Snowflakes are settling, without a sound.

Spring is coming, daffodils rise,
I can see the changes before my eyes,

Summer's arrived, the hot weather is here,
People having fun, let's all cheer!

Now it is autumn time, leaves are all around,
Bare branches on bare trees because the leaves are on the ground.

Back to winter now the four seasons have gone,
See you this time next year, so long!

Natalie Nunez (13)
Chelmer Valley High School

AUTUMN

The leaves fall onto the ground,
Gold, yellow, orange, brown,
Branches bare, people stare,
Autumn's here let's smell the air.

Children playing in the leaves,
Rustling, bustling, time for tea,
As I lie on my bed,
Thoughts of autumn in my head.

In the morning I awake,
I've got breakfast to make,
Autumn's gone, let's not cheer,
Instead we'll see a winter deer.

Joanne Piddington (12)
Chelmer Valley High School

LION

Once there lived a lion in the zoo
He was different from me and you.
Just between you and me
He's a very boring sight to see.
Even though the lion was boring and sad
He could go very mad.
He'd roar and bite,
He'd even once had a fight.
He'd pounce and claw,
And pace the floor
And roar a very loud roar!

Jamie Godden (12)
Chelmer Valley High School

Going Away

Today is the day,
When someone goes away,
Yesterday was the day,
When they were here to stay.

They're going today,
And nothing can stop them,
They stayed yesterday,
We had so much fun.

I'm going to miss them,
I wouldn't lie,
Today's the day,
We're going to say goodbye.

It can't be helped,
They're not around,
I feel like falling,
To the ground.

I'm very sad,
I'm all alone,
Today is the day,
They go back home.

Matthew Jarrett (12)
Chelmer Valley High School

Mysterious Box

I found a dusty, gloomy box mysterious and exciting,
Imagine what's inside it,
I sit and wonder could it be ancient, could it be old,
Could it be worth a lot of gold?

Dare I open the dusty box and find but nothing in it,
Or should I leave it for someone else to find,
And he who should find this mysterious box and feel the same as I,
And leave the box for someone else,
And ask themselves but why?

Carly Mann (12)
Chelmer Valley High School

A Poem For Princess Diana

The day was Saturday, it was sunny and bright,
cats were running around, active by day and sleeping by night.
People were sleeping, people were eating,
not a worry in the world, happy and gleaming.
But then the news came, there was shock and horror,
The Princess was dead,
First shock, then disbelief, then horror.

This couldn't happen, not to a Princess,
She was so warm and calm and kind.
Our thoughts go out to the children,
little Harry and Wills, they must be sad and empty inside.

The Princess was so special, so kind and normal, she was
the greatest by far.
Her death was so brave and painful, what a way to die.
The whole universe loved and worshipped her,
it was sad to see her die.
Millions of flowers, not a space in sight
People grieving day and night just to show they love her.
All the tributes, all the songs
The funeral is on Saturday and all the football's off,
but it will be worth it if Diana rests in peace.

Richard Jarrett (14)
Chelmer Valley High School

NEXT DOOR NEIGHBOUR

He lurks in the shadows of an old manor house,
His footsteps are as quiet as a mouse.
He never steps out into the burning hot sun,
He might not even know a new day has begun.

I sometimes hear his cries at night,
I can sometimes feel all his fright.
I sent him a letter about how he cried,
He sent *me* a letter,
He denied.

I hope to see him one day,
And talk to him about lots of things.
And really get to know him,
And become really good friends.

Holly Henry (12)
Chelmer Valley High School

THE SKUNK

Once upon a time,
There lived a little skunk,
He lived a very happy life,
But oh my God he stunk!

He lived in a little wood,
Just beside a barn,
He lived a very happy life,
And wouldn't do no harm!

He lived in a burrow,
Beside a little wall,
He lived a very happy life,
And couldn't care at all.

His horrid smelly, stink,
Kept away his enemies,
He lived a very happy life,
And lived anyway he pleased.

Richard Morgan (12)
Chelmer Valley High School

LOVE TRIANGLE

I have some love from me to you
But you won't accept my gift to you
My heart's in pieces for the love of you
Give me your heart, give me your soul
For I gave you mine
Put me at rest and give me your love
And I will be the happiest girl in the world . . .

But you took too long, long
And my love ran out
I was so wrong
To think I loved you
For I love someone else
And my love now is for eternity.

Katie Faramarzi (12)
Chelmer Valley High School

I DARE YOU!

I dare you to climb that tree,
I dare you to flick that pea!
I dare you to eat a worm,
I dare you to get a perm!

Play 'knock down Ginger',
You go first,
Why don't you?
I did the worst!

Dares, dares, dares,
That's all we do!
Eat a fly,
I dare you!

Hannah Miller (12)
Chelmer Valley High School

A RECIPE FOR AUTUMN

Take a stretch of woody land,
Sprinkle with red, orange, brown and
Add some blackberries here and there;
Mix in some conkers and squirrels too,
Then stir it together for a rich autumn stew.

Cassie Harvey-Smith (11)
Finchingfield Primary School

A SEA BREEZE

It is a hot summer's day
to quench my thirst I sip
a transparent glass of lemonade
whilst paddling in the tranquil sea . . .
The ice-cold water is refreshing as
it flows against my bare legs,
as a light breeze brushes my face
I look up at the sky and immediately
feel happy . . .
I can almost feel my eyes glistening
like crystal as I walk slowly
back to my beach towel -
in the dark, cool shade of
an umbrella.

Victoria Davies (12)
Frances Bardsley School for Girls

WHAT IS . . . ?

Relaxing like the mists off the Aegean Sea in the early
morning light,
Dolphins like shimmering silk diving up and down again,
Clear and smooth like freshly frozen pond ice
Sapphires and crystals sparkling under a bright fresh summer
morning sky,
Winter and rain and tall high mountains,
Ice, water and rain from the natural world around us,
And bubbles which float in the bath holding all the secrets
of the world.

Victoria Loomes (12)
Frances Bardsley School for Girls

SPELLBOUND

My small baby brother makes me spellbound,
He's so sweet and cuddly.
His fingers are so tiny,
And he has such small nails.
He takes his blue teddy everywhere,
And his large blanket too.
He laughs when I play with him,
But does not like baths as much.
I read him stories sometimes,
And he loves it when I do.
He's really very lovely,
And I love him lots and lots.

Jennifer Bull (11)
Frances Bardsley School for Girls

ICE

Once again I am free
The bitter coldness creeps
down my spine.
The soft trickle of water
touches my lips and a
vision of dolphins playing
in the waves sticks in my
mind.
Everything is silent, so still
and quiet.
Once again I feel free.

Natalie Thomas (12)
Frances Bardsley School for Girls

World Through The Window

It's February 1992,
My hands are cold,
My nose is blue . . .
I look out the window
It's crystal clear
voices of people, I know,
I hear.
As cold as ice are
my ears, with which
I hear
I step outside and
then I see
A frozen lake,
glistens like the sea.
A blast of icy wind
whips by
And then it's followed
by a lonely sigh.

Abida Siddiqi (12)
Frances Bardsley School for Girls

Spellbound By Boyz!

The Boyz that are totally gorgeous
Usually make us girls spellbound
with their charming blue eyes
and their irresistible smiles.
Everything they do makes us go *wow!*

Jade Stoner (11)
Frances Bardsley School for Girls

Oh How I Love Him

Oh how I love him,
How I love him dear,
He sits there smiling,
But not at me.
Oh why does he not notice me,
Oh why, what is it,
Love, what is love,
Is it good, is it bad,
Oh how I love him,
Love him I do.

Sarah Ann Rutland (11)
Frances Bardsley School for Girls

Spellbound

He had been struck down by a
witch's curse,
For better,
Or for worse.

Gone away was that brat,
Who all day long by the TV sat.

Now he is the witch's helper
Who follows her around all day to help her.

Nina Wallace (11)
Frances Bardsley School for Girls

Gently The . . .

Gently the lady put the baby to bed.
Gently the lady put a pillow under its head.
Gently the lady went to bed.
Gently the lady woke and heard a sweet cry.
Gently the lady crept to the cot.
Gently the lady rocked the cot.
Gently the baby fell asleep.

Leanne Bryan (11)
Frances Bardsley School for Girls

What Is Courage?

What is courage?
Is it a lion brave and strong,
Or is it a child trying something for
The first time?

What is courage?
A skydiver jumping from a plane,
Or is it a rock climber climbing a rocky cliff?

What is courage?
Is it to face your fear,
Or own up to something wrong?

Is courage fighting a fight,
Or walking away from it?

Is courage to stand up for yourself,
Or to run to safety?

Adrienne McCormack (12)
Gable Hall Secondary School

MEMORIES

The memories are strong yet my heart is not.
In the clear white snow we would talk alone.
Some nights I wonder what went wrong, others
I would pray for this pain to go away.
Little by little we grow apart, the love we once
had is no longer in our hearts.
It was all over in just a day, now that someone else
stands in the way.
I think of him a lot, will it ever stop?
The memories I will hold forever in my soul.
He used to care for my love, now our friendship has
vanished to dust.
Why does he treat me like he does?
What can I say to make him stop?
I want to be his friend can't he see, he blames me for
something only he can see. Friends are for life not a day
whenever he feels like it he will come my way.
Well not no more, those days have gone, he seems
to forget our love song.
Now there is no truth in your love, you use people
like no one does, still I won't forget the love you
once gave, forever and ever I will save.

Lisa Gardner (14)
Gable Hall Secondary School

WHAT IS COURAGE?

Courage is being brave and strong,
Courage is letting nothing go wrong,
Courage is doing something you have never done before.

You may be scared out of your wits,
Your knees are shaking, your belly feels sick,
As they tighten the rope around your waist

In two minutes' time it will be over,
you close your eyes, clench your teeth,
You feel this sudden urge then you go, go, go,
Till the people above you no longer see.

You see the floor,
As you reach the bottom, you breathe a sigh of relief.

Kirsty Beard (12)
Gable Hall Secondary School

Courage

Courage is to face up to your fears,
Courage will stay with you for years,
Face that fact,
don't go back.

Courage is to face up to your fears,
Courage will stay with you for years,
Like camping out
don't shout out.

Courage is to face up to your fears,
Courage will stay with you for years,
Firemen smell smoke,
so then they choke.

Courage is to face up to your fears,
Courage will stay with you for years,
From a sky diver,
to an ambulance driver.

Courage is to face up to your fears,
Courage will stay with you for years,
Drug dealers deal the pill,
They know drugs can kill.

Louise Ockendon (12)
Gable Hall Secondary School

Love!

As I hold you close in my arms
our lips linking,
like two lovers we melt together.
When your arm is
holding me close it's like a blanket
keeping me warm.
You've made me feel loved like
never before
And as you look into my eyes
the passion burns
through your eyes and into mine
and forever our love will
linger on!

Laura Fenneberg (14)
Gable Hall Secondary School

I Never Said Goodbye

He left without my knowing,
I came back and he was gone,
No more padding up the stairs
now I feel forlorn.
It happened Thursday night when I went out to play,
I came back in the morning he had gone away.
I won't have any more flea bites,
nor any more hair.
He has gone forever, it's my worst nightmare.
My dog went to the vet's. He could hardly walk.
Only my mum came back, I felt it was all my fault
I cried and cried and cried
I never said goodbye!

Helen Gillan (12)
Gable Hall Secondary School

HER FEELING

The feeling starts in her stomach
Then moves to her chest.
Through her pipes and over her heart,
Slowly crawling, slowly moving up.

Then the feeling moves to her neck
And travels to her downcast mouth
Up and up and up
Touching her nose, cheeks and eyes
Lastly the feeling reaches her brain.

In her body all the feeling stays
Until she thinks about the feeling
Then she shows the feeling in the
only way she can.

She cries

She knows the feeling
She knows the feeling's strength
She knows she's in pain
She knows she is hurting.

That is what I'm feeling
It won't go away
I know I'm in pain
I know I'm hurting.

Danielle Ireland (15)
Gable Hall Secondary School

Deadly Games

Rocketing down a main straight,
For the corner breaking late,
Taking someone with inches to spare,
These courageous people are full of dare.

Flicking up through the gears,
Increasing with speed,
To your utter disbelief,
You're in the lead.

You turn into the pits,
What an important time,
They jack you up,
And you're back on line.

There's five laps to go,
You're still in the lead,
There's a puff of smoke,
You reduce in speed.

You're on the last lap,
And just in front,
News from the radio,
There's been a shunt.

It's the second place man,
There's a sigh of relief,
You take the chequered flag,
With smiles and teeth.

You've won the race,
What an incredible feeling.
You lift the trophy,
The crowds are cheering.

Adam Russell (12)
Gable Hall Secondary School

A Wish

I lay there on the beach
The cool breeze blowing softly on my face
The sand as golden as the sun
And the fresh salty smell wafting
in from the sea.

I remembered when I was ill
That I had to take a lot of pills
I used to lay there motionless
in my hospital bed.
Wishing that one day I would play
again.

Now that day has come
What I had wished for had come true
There I was with my mum, Sue
my dad Drew.
And even my little brother Andrew.

All sitting there on the beach
I even ate a peach
My brother reached out to pull
me up
As I was holding a cup.

I had cancer, Oh how I wished to be
a dancer
Now my cancer has finally gone
And best of all the wish that I had
made on my 8th birthday to be a dancer,
was a dream no more.

Sam McQuade (13)
Gable Hall Secondary School

FIREMAN'S COURAGE

First day out on a call
Nervous, shaking, trembling like mad
But still determined to carry it out
And put that horrible fire out.

After this the chief goes in
To find out what's the cause.
He comes running out
Shouts run for your lives
The building's about to *explode!*

But sad to say, they didn't hear
And all the Blue Watch gang left dead!

The place was quiet
Lonely to say the least
All because of this horrible fire
These good people were just wiped out!

Stuart Mobsby (12)
Gable Hall Secondary School

THINGS THAT ARE NOT THERE

One bright day, when the sun had rose,
I got my shoes onto my toes.
Today I'll go for a walk, I thought,
I slipped out the back door,
To the wood I went.

The wood was dark and spooky,
A chill ran down my back,
My mouth was dry,
I chose to say goodbye.

I ran from the wood as fast as I could,
Seeing things that made me scared.
Ghosts and goblins,
Things that made me shiver.

I soon got home safe as could be,
But now I see,
That what I saw was not quite there,
And only existed in me.

Barry Page (13)
Gable Hall Secondary School

DREADED DETENTION

I know I shouldn't have done it.
I really did feel bad.
The teacher shouted one more time.
But when the teacher pulled a card out,
I could only read one word.
Detention!
I wanted the floor to swallow me up
This time I'd really crossed the line.
The very next day at twenty past three,
My friends all crowded around me.
'Are you going?' they all said.
I went to the room with a feeling of dread.
I wanted to be at home in bed.
The teacher looked up she saw me come.
I gave her the card.
In an hour I was on my way home.
I survived!
I'm not dead!

Maria Holland (13)
Gable Hall Secondary School

ABOUT A FIREMAN

Firemen are brave and save people,
once they saved a vicar from the steeple,
he was hanging by a rope.
The firemen came with some hope,
they don't know what to do,
so they're looking for some clues,
they went to the Pope,
and asked him.
He said he went to ring,
the bell.
It went ding, ding,
The firemen put a ladder up,
and they went up.
The vicar was tied up,
they untied him and he dropped.
The firemen said 'Oh no!'

Leanne Archer (12)
Gable Hall Secondary School

SHADOWS OF THE NIGHT

As I walked up the stairs to bed,
I had scary visions in my head.
The trees outside the window,
looked like monstery figures.
When I looked at them they gave me the
shivers,
but when I reached my bedroom and turned
on the light,
I realised they were not such a fright,
just shadows in the dark, mysterious night.

Naomi Wilson (12)
Gable Hall Secondary School

The Fire Engine

As I look at the window
Watching the fire engine
Stopping outside the burning building
Watching the firemen rush to the door

Pulling out the hose
Spraying into the fire
Then they send a ladder up
Rescuing the people from the building

Eventually they get the fire out
The people are OK
Within a few days
People are back as normal.

Lee Wightwick (12)
Gable Hall Secondary School

My Tent

I laid in my tent that cold winter's night,
All alone with no one in sight,
The moonlight shone through,
The air felt so cool.

Apart from an owl quietly hooting and the wind gently whistling,
The world seemed a silent place.
(Well, my garden did)

I drifted off to sleep with happy thoughts in my head,
When I awoke the next morning I remembered that I wasn't in my bed,
But I was in my trusty tent instead.

Mikaela Wakefield (12)
Gable Hall Secondary School

The Troll

I once went on a camping trip,
With my friend Pip
I was only six years old,
But for that age, I was very bold.

Into Condovers field we went,
To spend a night in a tent
I said 'This is going to be cool!'
To say this I was such a fool.

We had our cocoa and went to bed
Pip was scared, so he grabbed his ted
We lay down our heads to get some sleep
Pip rolled over into a heap!

At twelve o'clock, or about that
I felt a pushing on my roll-mat
The troll!
Or was it a mole?

It was a mole
When the tent came down, we saw the hole
The mole had come up for some air,
But couldn't, because my tent was there!

Jamie Percival (12)
Gable Hall Secondary School

A Courageous Poem

Courage is about being fearless,
Courage is about bravery.
People are courageous,
Like you and me.

A fireman is courageous, every day.
Saving lives by the dozen.
Although he does this for quite low pay.
He's back in time to see his cousin.

Matthew Guscott (12)
Gable Hall Secondary School

Relief Worker

I'm standing in a village
It's pouring with rain,
The skinny little children
Crying because of their pain.

I listen to the sound
Of the crying babies
Some have diseases
Like cancer or rabies.

I looked around
And felt sorry for the mothers,
Who had to find food
Or look after others.

I felt so unhappy
Knowing that they,
Were going through a famine
Nearly every day.

Laura Randall (13)
Gable Hall Secondary School

Courage Poem

Brave, selfless, courageous.
Firemen are all these.
They save old ladies from blocks of flats
And even cats up trees.

When fire extinguishers are not enough
They're always on hand to be there.
So, if you need some assistance
The firemen will always care.

He risks his life
To save you and I
He jumps into fires
Knowing he may die.

Louise Graves (12)
Gable Hall Secondary School

My Mate

My mate is called Sam
he has the power to stop a van
Well, at least he used to
until he caught a disease
He fights all day
smiling away
just dying for the pain
to go far, far away
He has kids but they don't know
'It's for the best,' he tells me
That's all I know.

Dean Maguire (12)
Gable Hall Secondary School

THE FIREMEN

Firemen are on call all day,
They travel a long, long way,
Saving cats from trees,
Sometimes burning their knees,
They always show courage,

Firemen show courage
In different ways,
Run to save the day,
Even I couldn't do it,
Maybe you could do it,
A lady sometimes does it,
Never mind I won't do it.

They show a lot of courage.

Kimberley Portas (13)
Gable Hall Secondary School

WHAT DOES COURAGE MEAN?

Courage means being brave,
It also means being strong,
There are many courageous people in this world,
Including firemen, policemen and more,
When little boys camp at night all alone,
And blind boys and girls can't see,
Hospital patients, perhaps dying in bed,
All these things take courage,
And we have all got it -
Both you and me.

Lara Sutherland (12)
Gable Hall Secondary School

Being Brave

What is courage?
When you face up to your fear,
I had to do that once,
went to an adventure park,
was with all my friends,
had to climb a 30ft wall,
am afraid of heights,
didn't want to be left out.
When I got going it was fun.

Michael Westley (12)
Gable Hall Secondary School

Courage

If you show courage you are brave,
What you do is save,
People from fires,
And cats from trees,
Firemen save many a day,
With only little pay.

Jodie Harrison (12)
Gable Hall Secondary School

I Thought You Were My Best Friend

I thought I could trust you,
I thought you liked me,
I thought you cared.
I thought you wouldn't lie to me.
I thought you would stick by me through thick and thin
I thought wrong and I know that you're not my best friend.

George McAllister (14)
Gable Hall Secondary School

School

I'll always remember my table,
Richard, Steve, Edwin and me.
The trouble we used to get into,
We always were laughing with glee.

Our classroom was bright, and luminous at night,
with our colourful paintings on the walls,
If you were lucky and your painting was good,
It might get pinned up in the hall.

The trouble with school was there's too much to do
that we never could fit it all in,
Half of the work that I proudly produced,
would end up in Mr Brown's bin.

Our class hatched some eggs and it took many weeks,
in a large orange incubator.
All eight of them hatched and we gave them all names,
but one of them died a bit later.

I always would fall and have scabs on my knees,
which I took great delight in picking.
I also like football which is such a great sport,
and involved lots of booting and kicking.

Break time was the best part of school,
and we'd always have a good play.
The bell would go ding when it was time to go in,
but we always would try to delay.

Robert Linham (16)
Havering VIth Form College

I, Myself And Me

You ask me who I am,
I say I am Sarah,
but you take away my name,
and you ask me once again.

You ask me who I am,
I say I am a daughter,
but you take away my parents,
and you ask me once again.

You ask me who I am,
I say I am a sister,
but you take away my brother,
and you ask me once again.

You ask me who I am,
I say I am a girl,
but you take away my gender,
and you ask me once again.

You ask me who I am,
I say I am a teenager,
but you take away my age,
and you ask me once again.

You ask me who I am,
I say I am a human,
but you take away my genus,
and you ask me once again.

You ask me who I am,
I say I cannot answer,
but you say I must,
and you ask me once again.

You ask me who I am,
I say I am me,
for I cannot answer your question,
and you won't ask me again!

Sarah Pym (16)
Havering VIth Form College

My Old Primary School

My old primary school will forever be a memory,
A compact, sweaty, uncomfortable classroom.
The smooth, shiny floor,
Wreaking of a strong, smelling disinfectant.
My friend, Jen, and I,
Reaching for the long window poles,
Enabling the room to fill with the fresh, lingering smell
Of our large green playing fields.
The noise becoming too much,
Crashing and banging carried through the door,
My concentration interrupted!
The screeching of the small, worn, white chalk
Against the old, dusty blackboard.
I hated those woolly tights,
They never matched my grey, pleated skirt
And creased, plain white shirt.
Noises echoing from the room next door,
Some lucky class were getting to watch the tele,
Still,
Not long to go,
Any minute now,
The noise everyone longed for,
Bouncing off every corner of the school,
The home time bell!

Maria Tyler (16)
Havering VIth Form College

A Stranger In A Big City

A blue sun rose in the yellow sky,
In the strange city of nowhere.
The clouds were pink, the grass white,
And a small black snake scurried into his tiny hole.
Orange dots hurry to their destinations,
Some on a strange creature travelling fast through tunnels,
Holding another over their shoulder or in their hands.
Some are big, some small, and some tiny in their elders' arms.
Some held symbols, maybe codes, on their backs.
Many orange dots approaching many temples at a time.
But then, there is quiet and nothingness around,
And emptiness surrounds the city of nowhere.
No feelings held in the hearts of lost souls,
No emotions visible in their eyes,
Nothing, I can make of the loneliness around,
The windows to their souls no longer stand for all to see.

Lucy Brace (16)
Havering VIth Form College

Confusion

Confusion is a sin, it's so full of vices,
With an aroma so strong, of Chinese herbs and spices,
Its taste is sharp, extreme and it stings,
Sweet and sour sauce on hot chicken wings,
My fingers can trace the rocky path of my mistakes,
Like broken concrete, with the cracks and crevices that it makes,
the sound is a symphony concerto, rising high,
But then quickly falling low, like an eagle, swooping in the sky,
My feelings are dolly mixtures and allsorts pouring from above,
Falling in their thousands in a tidal wave of love.

Melanie Wilkins (17)
Havering VIth Form College

Authority

A loud blast echoes from the distance
Signalling the arrival of something big
A strange musk fills the air
Odd smells flooding the senses
A huge creature rumbling forward
Complete disregard for all of its surroundings
Destruction accompanies its huge presence
All shall fall before its mass
But something strange comes with the beast
A coldness chilling the surrounding air
Its texture defies its smooth appearance
The roughness a strong contrast to its desired look
Its victims fall under its thunderous feet
After they have tasted its harshness
They go down as proof of what it wants
No one shall question its authority.

Matthew Hart (16)
Havering VIth Form College

Unconscious

A pale horse appeared,
Bearing a pale rider on his back.
I looked up at him, confused,
and I thought I saw him smile,
But he cannot smile.
I looked down to my feet and saw him.
I felt no remorse or anger
for I was no longer him.
A voice said, 'Come.'
And we walked away to a different place.

Colin Budge (16)
Havering VIth Form College

WHITEWASH

I close my eyes
to see the naked white walls
that looked so much bigger
when I was six.

And my mum
stroking her hair
trying to remove
the stains from the white paint.
It's grey hair really.
She smells of onions and there are tears streaking her cheeks
'Run your fingers under the cold water, mummy'
I tell her
but she says that
it won't work.

I can hear my brother
singing the Eastenders' song
with Mr Redwood.
And I know there is a window
somewhere
because I can see the light.

But before I go
I remember
me and James
hugging the walls
that we missed so much
after we went.

And when I open my eyes
again I realise the tears
are streaking my cheeks
and I know that
not even cold water
can save me now.

Anna Kristine (16)
Havering VIth Form College

When You Look At Me

Please see me as me,
Not as what you want me to be,
I am myself and will be forever,
An acting character I'll be never.

Please don't order and rule my life,
Sometimes I want to stab you with a knife.
I am responsible, there's no need to worry,
Remember you aren't me, you're only my mummy.

Please ask instead of tell,
Don't you know you're making my life hell.
You must remember when you were my age,
You're trapping me inside a locked cage.

Don't ask me to tidy my room one more time,
If you do I'll just annoy you and whine.
You know I hate greens, so why must I savour the flavour?
Why don't you shut up and do me a favour?

But when I look at you I feel something that's hard to find,
Despite all the grief and anger you still play tricks with my mind.
Somehow I always end up feeling bad when we argue,
But when I think about it, I guess that's just because I love you.

Louise Fairweather (16)
Havering VIth Form College

Pink, Plastic Lunch Box

Inside my pink, plastic lunch box are the remains of my past.
Smells of lunchtimes,
Echoes of innocent laughs,
Rotting leftovers of a ham and pickle sandwich,
Lovingly wrapped in foil by my mother,
And half a stale chocolate cake,
I gave my best friend the other half.

Inside my muddled and confused head
are memories of playtimes on the field,
Of dewed grass and children's laughs
Of spinning round and round and round and round,
Till I fall over on the soft grass,
Acorns and conkers by my nose
And watch the sky and clouds as they float past

Sarah Gonputh (16)
Havering VIth Form College

When You Look At Me

Please see me with your own eyes for what I really am,
Please don't see through another's eyes,
Please think what you wish to think,
Please don't think what another thinks,
Please ask your innermost thoughts,
Please don't ask another's thoughts,
And when I look at you it will be with my eyes, my thoughts and
my questions, not another's.

Rachael Eastwood
Havering VIth Form College

My Prize Possession

(I will never leave you, Teddy)

Warm fluffy socks,
and snugly big jumpers.
Sleepiness overcomes me.
I will never leave you, Teddy.

Outside in the garden,
wind howls through the trees.
Little black birds twitter,
collecting worms for their tea.

In the room next door,
the crash of cars,
the clink of metal.
My little brother acting out
the forces of good.

Downstairs in the kitchen,
mum prepares dinner.
Roast chicken and roast potatoes,
Chocolate pudding for afters.
The smells waft upstairs
and under my blanket.

Back in my secret den,
My cosy, warm den.
Jemima and I sleep,
resting our weary eyes.
Safe and still in the darkness,
I will never leave you, teddy.

Katherine Challis (16)
Havering VIth Form College

Game Play

A black veil hides the sky.
Plunging the world into darkness.
Inhabitants of earth stand in terror,
Gazing,
Clouds conflict above,
Crashing, torn like ripping flesh.
Seeping scarlet stained resin.
Continents scream.
Blood sectioned faces disperse in every direction.
The ground ruptures.
Red rivers run filtering through our demolishing earth.
Fear shudders through live corpses
Combustion spreads.
We become the fuel of hell's incinerator.
Raging flames eat our tortured earth.
The game-master grins;
He created the fear.
The atmosphere collapses,
Earth elapses in time
A vacuum is created.
The fiery screams of the world have no medium
Can they exist if there is no one there to hear them?
A delightful scowl spreads his face.
As hell on earth is created.
And earth has created hell.

Kelly Chesterton (16)
Havering VIth Form College

The Place That Dreams Are Made Of

Jars upon jars of children's dreams
towered above me.
The crisp paper bag sat in my hand
calling for those sugar dummies
which were within my reach.
Overwhelmed, I wondered where to go first.
My brother's eager fist, first to dive
into the sea of sweets.

Almost anchored by the jumper
that 'You'll grow into dear'
I shuffle, unsure, towards shelves stacked high.
How I'd love to taste
the tangy sweetness of cola bottles
placed between pastilles on the third shelf
which (my brother loved to remind me)
were rather out of reach.

George, stood tall as always,
behind the counter grinned.
The faint sound of a radio
played in the back room
strictly out of bounds.
A musty smell drifted out towards my nose.
As money clinked in the till
I wondered what was on forbidden ground.

Joanna Warwick (17)
Havering VIth Form College

YOU WILL ALWAYS BE REMEMBERED

(Dedicated to Diana, Princess of Wales)

You will always be remembered
Just like the first step a baby takes

You will always be remembered
Like the first blossom of the rose in spring

You will always be remembered
For the sunshine you've brought to everyone you met

You will always be remembered
As a beautiful treasure God loaned to us for a while

As we look and admire all the work you have done
They show a wonderful picture of a wonderful person,
Who cared, shared, and dedicated her entire life to helping people

Now and forever,
You will always be remembered.

Porsha Roache-Robinson (13)
Ilford Ursuline High School

IMAGINATION

Darkness can be mysterious,
Footsteps follow me through the night,
Whose they are, I cannot tell,
As darkness never reveal itself.

Imagination leads me astray,
That I'll never see another day,
It will come and tear me apart,
Open me up and rip out my heart.

Imagination has power to create,
The essence of darkness and feelings of hate,
To explore the mind and inner soul,
Fear or happiness forever to hold.

Meera Kataria (16)
Ilford Ursuline High School

Life As We Know It

Life has many friends,
But as time goes by, they drift from you as you sigh.
Life as well has its surprises.
For you may jump for joy or fail to be left to cry.
If you are strong you will succeed.
But if you are weak you will start to weep.
You may try to leap to your friends,
But shall fail, you need a little help along the way.
But try not to hold back in dismay.
A helpful hand will take you to your path, and there you shall
begin to start.
Life shall have its ups and downs.
But you will survive, take a deep breath and you shall win the test.
There is nothing more I have to say.
Except that my spirit is with you all the way.

Bobby Chowdhury (11)
Ilford Ursuline High School

PROMISE?

'She had so much to live for,'
I hear people say;
(Then why am I dead?)
The crowd of professional sympathisers
Gather round my family, trying to comfort them;
But words bring no comfort.

The epitaph,
My epitaph reads:
'Lived a short life, but a good one.'
Then why did I choose to take it away?
Nobody knows what life was like for me
The inner torments of my soul.

I had promise,
I wanted to conquer the world . . .
But talent isn't enough,
You need luck,
And I wasn't there when they handed it out.
My life was like a bottomless pit . . .
No matter where you go
You're no closer to fulfilling it . . .
So I chose my own finish,
My own claim to fame.
The dramatic ending that leaves the audience open-mouthed,
Still glued to the edges of their seats when the curtain goes down.
Well, it's one way of getting people to notice you;
Except you don't need the attention any more.
I never did get my curtain call!

Camilla Bhachu (15)
Ilford Ursuline High School

What Is Life?

What is life?
Is it a gentle thing, all calm and mild,
As lovely as a newborn child?
Or a wild teenager who dyes her hair blue,
Trying to see her heartbreak through?
Or an unemployed person with a family to support,
A pregnant woman who is about to abort?
Life is a hunter stalking its next victim.
Eyes burning and expression grim,
Longing to hear the anguished cries
Which are a result of people's deprived lives,
But life feels the power for precious little time
As death dawns near and life realises its crime,
What is life? I ask you again -
Life is for real, not a game.

Nishani Balendra (14)
Ilford Ursuline High School

HARVEST HOME

The tall combines stalk the fields,
Spewing corn and swirling dust.
The harvest mice
look and sigh
as they see the mechanical giants,
stomp up and down
until the crop they long to eat
is gone.

The air is warm,
The song, sweet,
The village church full,
The altar packed with goods for all,
and all the village praise the Lord,
for all is safely gathered in.

Eleanor Kirby (13)
Ilford Ursuline High School

CLOUDS

If you look in the sky on a sunny day,
What will you see coming your way?
Maybe a pig or a ball,
If you do, call,
Come on, my friends, what do you see?
Just look above you and me,
You might see the shape of a plane,
But there will never be two the same,
Clouds, clouds are so cool,
What can you make out of them all?

Victoria Jackson (12)
King Harold Grant Maintained School

At The Stables

Hooves making a tapping sound clip clop
along the ground.
In the field galloping around see their tails
swishing round.
Next day bring them in
ready for the ride to begin.
Get the saddle and bridle from the room,
riding hat and crop too.
Mounting on ready to go nudge on and of we go.
In the paddock trotting around
in a line there is a peaceful sound.
After a good day's ride
feed them hay
and groom them for a little a day.
Then do them hay bags and water for the rest
of the day.
Go home at 6pm
looking forward to next week again.

Danielle Cox (13)
King Harold Grant Maintained School

Football

Football, football, it's so cool,
I love it when I'm on the ball.

It's brilliant when we win the game,
no other feelings are quite the same.

After the game we celebrate,
that's why football is so great.

Tony Seary (12)
King Harold Grant Maintained School

The Wedding Reception

Girls in dresses,
Men in hats,
Some men skinny and some
men fat!
Coke on the table,
Wine in the glass,
The men drink their lager
while women just dance.
Groom on the dance floor
along with the bride,
But it's getting quite late
and now everyone's tired.
So everyone goes and the
hall is empty,
And the just married couple
zoom off in their Bentley.

Toni Brown (12)
King Harold Grant Maintained School

London City

London City, what a place!
An ugly smile within a skyscraper-scarred face.
Streets that go on for miles and miles.
With shops that sell unusual, weird styles.
Ant the trains are like our thoughts.
They race,
And the air they push breathes a sigh.
London's not a lonely place.
So why am I?

Joanne McPeake (14)
King Harold Grant Maintained School

END OF TERM

The last lesson of the last day of school,
Is the worst one of them all
All the children sit around,
Listening to the terrible sound,
Of the teacher droning on.
About whatever it says in the book,
No one even bothers to look,
Yes, there're only five minutes left,
Oh, no! He's gonna go on
About that computer theft,
'Class I'd like to draw your attention . . .'
Buzzz! The bell goes, the class cheers
Oh no, now he's threatening to give us a detention,
'Right, class dismissed,'
School's over, school's out,
All the kids scream, laugh and shout!

Victoria Ravenhill (13)
King Harold Grant Maintained School

DOLPHINS

Splashing here
Splashing there
Splashing nearly everywhere
Some are blue some are grey
Flipping their fins
They're off and away.

Claire Newman (12)
King Harold Grant Maintained School

When Autumn Comes

When autumn comes
The leaves are
falling
falling
falling
Down to the ground
The squirrels hibernate
Through the winter to
The spring
When the leaves on the
Trees are sprouting.
The birds are singing
The chicks are chirping
And all the new
Plants are growing.

Martin Burr (12)
King Harold Grant Maintained School

I Wish

I wish I had her pale, red lips,
I wish I had her clever fingertips,
I wish I had her determination,
I wish I had her imagination,
I wish I had her skilful mind,
I wish I had her beautiful eyes,
I wish I had her creative hands,
I wish I had her tender skin,
I wish I was my mum.

Andrea Cave (12)
King Harold Grant Maintained School

The Big Match

Fans are at the turnstiles
But the queue is standing still
Spurs have got the Gunners
I hope they win six nil.

At last the queue is moving
And we all pack in the stands
The players run on to the pitch
I wish the whistle would blow.

The referee, he flips a coin
Yes! Spurs have won the toss
Two short spurts from the whistle
The game is finally off!

The game is hard for both sides
The teams defends well
The first half is a battle
Who'll win? No one can tell.

The second half has started
Ginola dribbles then stops dead
Makes a swift pass across to Ferdinand
Who kicks it right past Seaman's head

The crowd goes completely crazy
Chanting Spurs songs for their team
Then the final whistle blows
Spurs one - Arsenal nil

John Hall (12)
King Harold Grant Maintained School

Drug Taking

Don't be a drugs user today
you could be throwing your life away.
People drinking and taking drugs
are stealing to pay for the stuff.
Drugs will lead you into a life of crime
just to get another fix, just in time.
Drug addiction will lose your friends
and it will lead you to a dead end.
Glue-sniffing when you are young
will spiral out of control before you know.
Keep away from drugs, quit today.

Luke Power (12)
King Harold Grant Maintained School

The Seashore

The seashore so calm
like a fancy that goes on and on
but the whispering in the air
oh I do declare
the way the fish swim
happily the waves wash onto
the rocks
When I come here
it releases my soul
the seashore how great it is
you just can't ignore
its charm.

Jade Fitzjohn (12)
King Harold Grant Maintained School

DREAM

I went to bed at half-past ten
had a dream
all about me
I was playing basketball
for Orlando Magic
I got the ball and
showed my flair
I jumped and twisted eight times
in the air,
Just as I was dunking on
Michael Jordan's head,
my mum woke me up
because I fell out of bed!

Adam McInerney (13)
King Harold Grant Maintained School

ARABIAN SPIRIT

She stands noble
Her long mane blowing in the breeze
This free spirit of the
Arabian desert
Moves with such elegant ease
Her beauty and her speed
Are there for all to see
She is kind and gentle
She?
Is my horse.

Emma Ward (12)
King Harold Grant Maintained School

My Dream

Football football every day
I can't relax till I start to play
Alan Shearer on a run
David Beckham having fun
Half time comes
Still no goal
Then I score
I'm on a roll
The crowds are cheering
'We want more'
The atmosphere's electric
I'm lifted off the floor
Then lights start flashing
My eyes do stream
Bells are ringing
What is that noise?
I don't believe it
It's just a dream!

Christopher Gough (13)
King Harold Grant Maintained School

Buster

There was a dog called Buster,
Who used his tail as a feather duster,
As he walked round the room,
Using his nose like a broom,
He made the room all clean,
But as it sparkled and gleamed,
He sneezed all over the lot!

Kayleigh Westall (12)
King Harold Grant Maintained School

Whales

Whales are lovely mammals
swimming around in the sea
for such heavy bodies
they swim so gracefully
their huge tails lift and fall
making waves all around.

They spurt out water for all to see
for they are happy and full of glee
unaware of the dangers that lurk
for man will soon be here to do his work.
Come the fishermen in their boats
followed by a big wave and they got soaked
they set the harpoons at the ready
the men are feeling calm and steady.

The hunters know they need this whale
payment will bring food to their tables
the mammal is well within their sights
they fire the harpoon and score a hit.
A loud wailing cry and the whale fights
but its huge body is of no help.
Could this be the end of years of play
the hunters cheer and wave
today had been a very good day
for them.

Nicola Smith (12)
King Harold Grant Maintained School

FISHING

I like fishing
pulling up the rod
pulling it back
casting out
waiting for the fish
to take the maggot
seeing the float go up and down
taking the fish by surprise
hooking the fish
reeling in
weighing the fish
watching the scales go round
seeing the weight on the scales
unhooking the fish
and putting it back
seeing it swimming away
seeing if it's the catch of the day
taking the money
and going away.

James Schroder (13)
King Harold Grant Maintained School

HUNTED

Whale oh whale why
must it be you?
You're hunted for meat
and for your skin too!

If it weren't for the
public as your supporters,
the poachers' greed wouldn't
have altered.

I am proud of the
people for what they
have done,
if it wasn't for them
they'd hunt for fun.

Whether it's for skin,
meat, female or male,
the point is they're still
hunting whales.

Nina Maffei (12)
King Harold Grant Maintained School

BAN ANIMAL TESTING

Nasty things go on in the test lab,
Things that I really despise.
Things so cruel that if you saw them,
They would definitely make you cry.

Scientists wearing lab coats,
Picking up little white mice.
Tying them up so they can't move,
And rubbing shampoo in their eyes.

Drugs are tested on animals,
To see if they are a cure.
But is this any excuse,
For the suffering the animals endure?

So next time you buy some make-up,
Or a bottle of shower gel,
Think of the nasty experiments,
And the animals who went through hell!

Hazel Stelzner (13)
King Harold Grant Maintained School

Smoking Is One Bad Thing!

Smoking seriously damages
your wealth
Twelve milligrams of tar
and one milligram of nicotine
will lessen your health.
One packet a day that's
all you need,
While you're buying them
think of those in need!
All they do is cause your
cancer rate to increase,
If you stop now maybe it
will decrease.
I don't know why these
health hazards are made.
I bet the greedy makers and
sellers don't think about the
cancer victims in their graves.
Tobacco is a drug that should
have been extinct,
Instead it's still with us so
that some of us become
extinct!

Latoya Johnson (13)
King Harold Grant Maintained School

WRITE A POEM . . .

Write a poem about
anything they said.
So I tried and I tried
until it was time
for bed.
It took me all evening
to make something
rhyme,
But it was all rubbish
I'd been wasting my
time.
I thought of a rhyme
just before I went to
sleep,
But in my mind it
would not keep.
I woke in the morning
but my ideas were
dead,
Write a poem about
anything they said!

Jennifer Davis (12)
King Harold Grant Maintained School

MOVING HOUSE

Dark and dreary
In an empty room
In the doorway shadows lie
Moving silently
In a blink of an eye.

Rachel Boulton (11)
King Harold Grant Maintained School

Dad

Sunday morning
And I hear Dad snoring
Oh it can be boring
Waiting for breakfast
But I daren't wake him
He says 'Never wake a
Sleeping man'
So I pretend the snoring
Is just a lion roaring
Starving for red meat
Or anything to eat
And the roaring gets
Nearer and clearer
Out in the hall!
And so I call
'Dad!'
At last
We have breakfast.

Joanna Farley (13)
King Harold Grant Maintained School

Grandfather

(Dedicated to Ted Collins)

Days and nights go by,
I lay in my bedroom and cry,
Thinking about the day,
My grandfather stepped away.

He lived a joyful life,
Until one terrible day,
He knew it was his time,
To finally pass away.

Every now and again,
I go up to his grave,
To take a bunch of flowers,
And to express my pain.

I wish it'd never happened,
On that terrible day,
That my grandfather decided,
To finally pass away.

Tiffany Harold (12)
King Harold Grant Maintained School

ALIENS

Some people think aliens don't exist
but some people do

Now this is my story that happened
to me and might just happen to you

I fell asleep silently one night and
suddenly awoke by a flashing light.

There in front of me stood a strange
little creature

He talked in a funny language
which they call Keacher

Then we went far far away where
aliens were only allowed to play

I didn't stay there very long as the
smell on their planet was quite a pong

Now this is a story that did come true
and I think they'll be on their way for you!

Georgina Brant (12)
King Harold Grant Maintained School

Shopping

Gucci, Versace or Chanel,
I like names can't you tell?
Armani, Karen or maybe Klein,
On my credit cards I shall sign.

Shop, shop until I drop,
Oh yes I like that top,
Money flying here and there,
I think I'll sit down on this chair.

To Harvey Nichols I'll go now,
You never know there could be a sale,
Lots of bags have attached to me,
There will be more wait and see.

Yves Saint Laurent or Ralph Lauren
Oh no here I go again.

Lucy Bridges (14)
King Harold Grant Maintained School

My Baby Cries

Lying on the settee beside me,
My baby cries.
I look from my book and put it down.

This is no quick cry. She rages.
I lift her from where she lies,
Carry her about the room,
Talking nonsense endlessly.

She hears but not listens as
We walk from wall to wall, she rages on,
Loving her helplessly.

Lisa Flaxton (14)
King Harold Grant Maintained School

THINGS I LIKE TO DO

I like football and fishing too,
the biggest I've caught is bigger than you.

I ride my bike over a jump,
I got a puncture and needed a pump.

I like skating down steep hills,
but always remember speed kills.

I like rugby for the rough and tumble,
over the try line I like to stumble.

I play tennis at a very fast pace,
my opponents I like to ace.

Those are the things I like to do,
I think I'll go and play a few.

Josh Knights (13)
King Harold Grant Maintained School

DINNER

Once at dinner,
My mum got mad,
And threw a sausage roll,
At my dad.
My dad got angry,
And threw another,
And hit my brother.
My brother thought it was me,
And I got hit with another three.

David Hoye (13)
King Harold Grant Maintained School

The Condemned

Cold walls line a fortress
smelling of death,
Innocence whispers in a
soft breath
A shadow casts across a
dozen dreams
It's my fate yet others scream.

Was no other's life such a waste?
For there's only one way to leave
this place.

Through death's door the
people wait
To witness this distasteful fate.
So, take my heed as best you can
For I die an innocent man.

Maria Savill (13)
King Harold Grant Maintained School

Golf

I went to the golf course,
Got a hole in one,
But on the very next hole,
Got one hundred and one,
I broke my club,
By throwing it down,
I got so embarrassed,
And had to leave town.

Adam Taylor (13)
King Harold Grant Maintained School

The Dream

Tears are rolling down her eyes,
She is depressed, but in disguise.
She will wait and pray,
Until the day,
The day he comes,
To take her away.

She's off to a place with flowers
and butterflies,
She will sit there amazed and
flutter her eyes.
She is sitting there staring at
a beautiful scene,
Thinking 'This is where I must
have been.'

Lisa Cashman (14)
King Harold Grant Maintained School

The Aztecs And The Spanish

Swords are swinging
Shields are shining
Swords are killing
People are dying
The Aztecs are brave
The Spanish are bold
All this fighting was
Over some gold.

Shelley Webb (13)
King Harold Grant Maintained School

What Is Bullying?

Bullying is horrible,
Bullying is bad.
What is the point,
In making people sad.
Calling them names,
Like 'the freak',
Kicking and thumping,
Until they're beat.
They rip their clothes.
They steal their money,
Somehow they think that's funny.
Someday I hope they realise this,
That bullying is not bliss.

Gemma Lowe (13)
King Harold Grant Maintained School

The Haunted Forest

Deep in the woods on a very dark night
A ghost came out and gave me a fright
It made funny faces and funny noises
as well
It ran away and made a bad smell
It chased me through the forest and
up the stairs and then I saw a monster
with lots of hairs.
It came up to me and then went 'Boo'
I gave it a kick and it went down the loo.

Chris Martin (12)
King Harold Grant Maintained School

Summer To Winter

Summer is gone winter's nearly here.
If it starts to snow, you'll hear a
big cheer.

There'll be no more sun, there could
be a storm.
If you go outside wrap up warm.

The wind will be blowing, the sun
won't be shining,
If it starts to rain, kids will be
whining.

When it starts to snow there'll be
a snowball fight.
The children scream with laughter
and fright.

The snow starts to melt, the snowman
is going.
All you can see is his carrot
nose showing.

Olivia Dunne (13)
King Harold Grant Maintained School

A Poem

This poem is going to rhyme
I like writing poems all the time
Poems that are short, poems that are long
You can turn a poem into a song
Now I'm going to end this poem
So see you later now I'm going!

Sally Pritchard (12)
King Harold Grant Maintained School

The Storm

Crash goes the thunder
Lashing down the rain.
Crack goes the lightning
Again and again.

Clouds roll over
As thunder claps again.
Up goes the umbrella
To keep off the rain.

Then the storm is over
Puddles on the ground.
The sky is becoming brighter
Just wetness all around.

Sadie Stares (12)
King Harold Grant Maintained School

Winter's Coming

When I look out my window
The weather is slowly changing

The sunlight is fading
The darkness shading
And the squirrels hibernating
The leaves are falling
The flowers crumbling
The early evenings
The storms and the rain

Prove that winter's coming.

Daniel Coghill (13)
King Harold Grant Maintained School

FLY, FLY FROM ME

Fly, fly, fly from me,
The wind will take you across the sea,
Past the planets and the stars,
You must leave this world of ours.

You must fly away from here,
Leave this world of hope and fear.
The moon will rise and the sun will set,
But for me I'll never forget.

Now it's time to let you go,
You must leave here, that I know.
No more will I hear you laugh and sing,
Nothing's changed but everything.

I see your teardrops like the rain,
While you have been through all this pain.
So now it's time to say goodbye,
The world's still here and so am I.

Robert Elliott (15)
King Harold Grant Maintained School

THE TELEPHONE

I love the telephone,
I use it all the time,
I love to dial the numbers,
And hear the different chimes,
I love to talk to people,
Just before I dine,
Then I feel just fine,
The telephone is always
On my mind.

Emily Gapes (12)
King Harold Grant Maintained School

STARS

I sit and look at the sky at
night,
and wonder why that ball of
light,
took so long for us to see,
that does not make much
sense to me,
I wonder what it's like on Mars
to sit and look at
all those
stars.

Lisa Gubbings (12)
King Harold Grant Maintained School

THE SPIDER

Spider in the bathroom
Spider in the hall
Spider in the kitchen
I can't stand it at all
Then he's in my bedroom
I nearly had a fright
And then he crawled all
over me
In the middle of the
night.

Charlotte Thompson (12)
King Harold Grant Maintained School

FOOTBALL

There was once a boy from Lyme
Who scored a goal for his very first time
Although he was glad
His team mates were sad
'Cos he'd forgot to change ends
at half time.

Paul Jackson (12)
King Harold Grant Maintained School

PLAYING

Playing in groups, shooting some hoops
Playing about, running with a shout
Jumping up high, reaching for the sky
Playing with cars, looking at stars
Having some fun, playing with a squirt gun
You can go for a ride, have a smile with pride
It's just great, especially with a mate
Bikes going round bends, it just never ends.

Tim Hempsted (11)
King Harold Grant Maintained School

COMPUTER GAMES

Computer games are my pride and joy
Although I have a cat who likes to sit and watch me
And sometimes lends a paw
Together we kill aliens and travel through the door
Me and Coco shoot baddies in a game called Doom
Maybe he thinks we will stop them from getting in the room.

Edward Stelzner (11)
King Harold Grant Maintained School

NEW YEAR

December the 31st we all cheer,
because at 12 o'clock we start a
New year.
Big Ben strikes 12 we're all having fun
Happy New Year shouts everyone.
Party poppers pop we sing
'Auld Lang Syne.'
Everyone here is having a good time.
New Year's resolutions we all make,
The new calendar goes up and we
all eat some cake.
Early hours of the morning we all
go to bed,
and think about the year that's ahead.

Nicola Bull (13)
King Harold Grant Maintained School

THE JOURNEY

I cross the road by day or night,
I always forget to look left or right,
I begin my journey from one side
to the next,
It takes me so long with my small
little legs,
I stop in the middle to take a break,
I see a light and roll up tight,
I'm glad to get to the other side,
It's another trip in my hedgehog life.

Lorraine Keogh (13)
King Harold Grant Maintained School

Rainbows In The Air

It should be dark for it is night,
but look at the sky, it's full of light.
Gold dust sparkling everywhere,
shattered rainbows in the air.
Shrills and bangs and lots of noise,
scaring little girls and boys.
Fires roaring, blazing high,
help to light up all the sky.
But please be careful or it could be,
that for some it ends in tragedy.
Just take care and always remember,
the code for the night of the 5th of November,
And try to enjoy the magical sight,
of beautiful colours on this special night.

Pamela Sideras (12)
King Harold Grant Maintained School

Autumn Leaves

Autumn leaves gold and brown
The wind will blow
They all fall down
The sound of the crackling
Under your feet
As you walk down the cold
And windy street
Autumn is over
It's winter time
Now let's make a whole
New rhyme.

Dean Godtschalk (13)
King Harold Grant Maintained School

WINTER SEASON

It's winter now the birds huddle silently
on the window-sill.
It's turning really cold and the children's frosty
breath fills the air.
Throwing crumbs to birds, and watching them
feed - hungrily.

Winter comforts you by sitting on a chair
near to a window,
watching the snowflakes fall down to the
ground - silently.

Winter comforts you with a cup of tea,
I'm drinking it thinking about the future,
how it's going to be - dreamily.

Miyase Dogan (13)
King Harold Grant Maintained School

THE OLD GEEZER

The man next door is called Mr Small,
We kicked our football over his wall,
So I volunteered to get it back,
He said to me 'In my day I'd get a good whack,'
He's a grumpy old geezer with no respect at all,
'Oops, oh no I'm not getting the ball,'
My mate looked over the wall,
There sitting in his chair, was Mr Small.
My mate chucked over a brick,
It hit him on the head,
When I looked over the geezer was dead!

David Fisher (13)
King Harold Grant Maintained School

HALLOWE'EN

Hallowe'en comes but once a year,
To fill us all with dread and fear,
Witches on broomsticks in the sky,
On Hallowe'en I wish I could fly,
Children go from door to door,
And ask for treats and even more,
They all dress up and look so good,
To terrorise the neighbourhood.
Please don't worry,
Be content,
For no true harm is really meant,
There are no ghosts,
There are no ghouls,
To believe all this,
We must be fools.

Sarah King (12)
King Harold Grant Maintained School

FUNFAIR

I'm off to the funfair, for a good day out,
And when I get there I hear screams and shouts.
I see all my friends with their mouths open wide,
As they're screaming with laughter on the waltzer ride.
After the dodgems I get some chips,
Then we all run over to the crazy whip.
The ghost train's next for a scary ride,
And all our faces look terrified!
The last stop is the stall called the coconut shy,
We all quickly have a go and say 'Goodbye.'

Clare Simper (13)
King Harold Grant Maintained School

If I Were An Animal

If I were an animal I would want to be a dog
Because they're cuddly and furry and they sleep
like a log
I'd want to have a kind owner who would provide
everything I need
And so my owner wouldn't lose me I'd be on a lead
If I needed comfort I'd get on the settee
And if I wanted a branch to chew I'd bark up a tree
If I needed cuddling I'd beg like a tramp
And if I needed to watch the TV I'd sniff the dusty switch
And if I wanted scratching I'd fake I'd got an itch
That's why I'd love to be a dog.

Paul Clarke (12)
King Harold Grant Maintained School

Me

I have a little sister
Her name is Chelsea-Leigh
I also have two brothers
Who are always bothering me.

They cry and whinge,
And pull my hair.
So it seems to me,
They just don't care.

I wish they'd go away
I wish they'd disappear
But really deep down inside
To me they are so dear.

Kirsty Conlon (11)
King Harold Grant Maintained School

The Nursery Rhyme

The man in the fish shop,
Gave me a fish,
I went to thank him and
Then put it on a dish,
I went home at seven,
And put it in the oven,
When it was ready,
It tasted like heaven.

Samantha Ball (13)
King Harold Grant Maintained School

Magic

My idea of magic doesn't have much to do with stage tricks and illusions - the whole abounds in magic. When a whale plunges out of the sea like a newborn mountain, you gasp in unexpected delight. What magic! But a toddler who sees his first tadpole flashing in the mud puddle feels the same thrill. Wonder fills his heart, because he has glimpsed for an instant the playfulness of life.

When I see the clouds whisked away from a snowcapped peak, I feel like shouting, 'Bravo!' Nature, the best of all magicians, has delivered another thrill. She has expected the real illusions, our inability to be amazed by her wonders. Every time the sun rises, Nature is repeating one command: 'Behold!' Her magic is infinitely lavish, and in return all we have to do is appreciate it.

What delight Nature must feel when she makes stars out of swirling gas and empty space - she flips them like spangles from a velvet cape, a billion reasons for us to awaken in pure joy when we open our hearts and appreciate all she has given us, Nature finds her reward. The sound of applause rolls across the universe and she bows.

Chris Valentine (16)
Marshalls Park School

Hobbies!

My hobbies are things I enjoy,
There's flute, trombone and that new toy,
But best of all is dance and theatre,
'Young Generation' is my boredom beater.

At summer school, we had lots of fun,
We worked hard too and produced 'Annie Get Your Gun',
For my part I sang and danced a tap duet as Winnie,
I'm glad there's not a Disney show, I'd probably get Minnie!

At Christmas time, we've changed the style to
'Gilbert and Sullivan',
They wrote lots of musicals 'Hot Mikado' is one of them,
There's Nanki-Poo and Katisha, Pish-Tush and Koko Too,
If you enjoy fun, comedy and dance, this show's the one for you!

Hollie Kemp (14)
Rainsford High School

My Best Friend . . .

I have a friend, she really does care,
We have a lot in common - we make a great pair,
Everything we do, it is always together,
I know we will be friends tomorrow and forever.

She listens to me and helps me out,
I tell her my secrets without any doubt,
She brightens up sad rainy days,
She never has anything bad to say.

We never argue we never fight,
Our friendship will always glow like a light,
If I hadn't have known her for the last year,
My life would have been lonely and full of fear.

My best friend knows who she is,
To say a huge thank you I wrote this,
All my friends mean a lot to me,
But this one friend, in my mind I always see.

Sarah Allison (14)
Rainsford High School

Curiosity Killed The Cat

Curiosity killed the cat.
Wrong!
The cat in question was actually rather old,
He'd been left out in the rain that night and caught cold.
The next day he got stung by a bee,
And carelessly thrown off somebody's knee.
He'd been chased down the road by Lurcher the dog,
And funnily enough fell off a log.
Then there was the incident with the Hoover,
Well, the cat just wasn't a fast enough mover!
It was really bad luck which caused the cat's death,
An unfortunate end, but the truth none-the-less.

Anna Bateson (15)
Rainsford High School

In Line

I stand in line,
Everyone discussing how great it is going to be,
I am queuing here for my death,
A country so calm and peaceful,
Now evil and at its worst,
Why am I standing here?
My family and friends,
Left behind,
Lying dead in a trench,
No one knows this,
No one,
I must stop thinking this,
I sign my name,
In red ink,
Colour of blood,
My childhood memories flooding back,
As fast as a gunshot,
I might come back,
One in a million,
There is a small voice in my head,
It keeps repeating,
You do not know what you have got until it has gone,
I cannot turn back,
Not now,
Not ever . . .

Michelle Levene (13)
Rainsford High School

The Ballad Of Old Man Tom

The Apney Wood was haunted, and many folk did know,
That old man Tom he died there, and there no one should go.

One day two girls came walking, right through those Apney Woods,
They didn't know the story, that to go there no one should.

Tom's spirit looked and saw them, and then disaster struck,
Their screams were heard for miles, but right there they were stuck.

To great surprise of townsfolk, the girls came strolling out,
They laughed and told a joke, but people didn't doubt,

That old man Tom he had them, for through the girls' sweet smiles,
The evil spirit lurked about, and told so in their eyes.

Old man Tom had broken the curse, that in the woods he'd stay,
Until two girls who'll set him free, came walking there by day.

The wood now was not haunted, but in the town Tom lay,
The people fled for miles and went away to stay.

The town lay still and quiet, until some settlers came,
They all knew that he lurked there, yet still they came the same.

But soon to their shock horror, people they disappeared,
They knew that Tom, he had them, but how, what, when and where.

A young prince came to try him, and in the dark of night,
They had a great and mighty fight, the prince won fair and right.

The moral of this story, it really goes to show,
That good wins over evil, yet either never go.

Carla Wise (13)
Rainsford High School

ALONE ON THE HILL

Alone on the top of a hill,
Solitary at all times,
I cannot free myself from this place,
This hill is my home for all of eternity,
I am forced to change as the weather does,
Alter as all four seasons in a year pass,
I watch the colourful sunsets,
The breaking of a new day,
As the earth revolves.
I evolve to be the same,
But I am special,
As the thing that I am,
I am unique,
Alone on the top of a hill,
Solitary at all times,
I cannot free myself from this place,
As a seed I was planted here,
As a large oak tree I will stay.

Shona Hales (15)
St John's C of E School

GRABBED AGE AND YOUTH

Age is a wealth of knowledge,
Youth is an age of clubbing,
Age is a memory of the past,
Youth is for the future,

Youth is for dreams,
Age is full of sleepless nights.
Youth is one long summer
No rain,
Age is winter, dark and pain,

Life stands still, old and aged,
Youth strides on to fill life's pages,
But in time youth will age
And once more life will fade,
Life is a roundabout
Of youth and age.

Rachel McCue (12)
St John's C of E School

The Mind

A memory floats to the surface of a tranquil lake
Lazily it skims reality
Occasionally being immersed by tangled thoughts now long forgotten.
Beams of consciousness
Fall between the rich green leaves of silent morals
In which the dust of the past whirls
An everlasting cyclone
Of half-truths.
As with the first flush of spring or youth
The memory blooms.
As the crease in time is smoothed
The truth is understood
And the plug of rich, fragrant earth is removed
The wound is uncovered and the blood moves freely once more
Washed by a flow of sparkling tears
Which run forth, unchecked
Down furrowed cheeks
As light blooms from the dark of lies.
Time heals all wounds
But I would rather live in the shade of untruths
Than know of the cruelty and deceit of my fellow man.

Rosalind McGuire (15)
St John's C of E School

My Little Friend, In His Little World

Squirt,
That's my goldfish.
He lives in my glass fish tank,
Two feet wide, by one foot tall,
That's his own little world.

Did you ever wonder,
What they think about,
All day, every day,
In a little glass tank,
Two feet wide, by one foot tall.

Imagine eating only when fed,
Seeing day, only when your light is switched on,
And breathing clean air only when it's cleaned.
In your own little tank,
Two feet wide, by one foot tall.

Imagine being reliant on someone else,
All day, every day,
With not even a memory,
Of where you came from.
Just the memory,
Of your own little tank,
Two feet wide, by one foot tall,
Your own little world,
Now aren't you lucky?

Jennifer Cordell
St John's C of E School

UNDER THE SHADOW OF NIGHT

As I gaze across the dark, black void,
A space stretching to infinity
Yet is, in reality so near.
You dance, twirling around
And around this way, that way
In and out, down and then up again
Whilst the music plays. I don't hear
The words, the beat, the instruments, all I
Hear is the melody, sweet and loving,
Played with passion and desire.
The music fades, you lift up your eyes, with your
Smile, a small dimple appears in your left cheek.

I can't bear to be so near to you,
Yet not able to reach out and hold you.
I turn and walk away. Outside
It is raining. My tears mingle
With the falling rain,
My legs can no longer support me. I sit
On the wet grass, hug my knees,
Take deep breaths, One day, one day
Maybe you'll remember me.
Until then, I will watch over you,
Never will I stop loving you,
My child, my beautiful child.

Karen Hurley (15)
St John's C of E School

SCHOOL

Every day, when I go to school,
I think of how it's so uncool.
The first boring lesson has to be German
Lots of words, we have to learn 'em.
In maths there's a mega hard sum,
And under every table is hardened chewing gum.
For afternoon break the bell goes ding-dong,
But when I enter the toilet, there is a terrible pong.
My smell organs feel as if they are about to burst,
Out of all odours, this is by far the worst.
In English we have to write a play,
The worst thing we've had all day.
In PE we play a rubbish game,
Running around, which is ever so lame.
At school, what do we possibly gain?
I am never going back there ever again.

Kunal Patel (13)
St Nicholas School

THE TIGER

The tiger looks like glinting grass in the sun,
His fiery orange coat is as shiny as satin,
His dark menacing eyes catch the deer grazing.
He waits for the right moment,
Then *'whoosh'*,
He pounces on the deer.
The graceful but deadly predator
Bites the deer in the neck *'fang'* deep.
The helpless animal tries to struggle away,
But no luck.
It dies in pain.

Victoria Marnoch (12)
St Nicholas School

LIQUIDIZER-ANTEATER

Strong as a lion, eats like a pig,
There is the liquidizer with its sharp teeth.
It chews, it mashes, there's nothing to do,
As it comes nearer, nearer to you.
It stank of rotten food,
Its teeth were badly yellowed.
There was smoke from the plug.
The liquidizer looked a bit mellow.
The liquidizer roared furiously.
I heard it, and came to look, curiously.
It had obviously gone wrong, but how?
The shopkeeper said that it was designed to impress,
Maybe the plug went wrong, maybe the fuse.
Then I noticed something was wrong, gone,
Something called booze.
Hey, people heard the news.
Liquidizer caught, drinking booze.

Simon Black (13)
St Nicholas School

TWISTER

Over the horizon
Swooping and diving
Floating and gliding
High in the air
Suddenly plummeting down.
Then twisting up high.
Swooping and looping,
Gliding gracefully across the sky
Then plunging down
To a fluid landing.

Emma Goodfellow (13)
St Nicholas School

Cat And Mouse

He crept carefully over the dark laid back lane,
He ploughed through the grass like a tractor,
He came to a halt after hearing the fluttering of birds.
The skidding of a car startled the cat.
He rushed past the shrubbery and into a bush,
Then after about ten seconds, his head appeared out of
the thick grass.
Triangular, with button eyes and spiked ears,
He spotted a baby mouse dashing across the lane,
Then darted across after him.
The small brown rodent ran into a hole.
The cat was running after him rapidly.
The cat crept up to the hole;
Scrape! Scrape! The hole caved in.
Dragged him across the lane,
His legs pointing up towards the sky.
He took nibbles from his oval body,
And laid him on the side of the lane.

Bradley Exall (13)
St Nicholas School

In The Deep

His tail whirls around and around
But suddenly he surges forward
Menacing to all around

He glides forward like a predator
Popping out his eyes
Looking out of his periscope to see
What fun he can find

He's the emperor of all around
Loud yet proud
Roaming his territory
Elegant and majestic.

Zahra Paliwala (13)
St Nicholas School

THE FOX AND THE CHICKEN

A fox crept cautiously in the farmyard,
He was sly and clever.
He moved sharply through the tall thin grass
Breathing heavily.
There was something creepy and strange about him.
He came to a white fence,
He rested before the murder was to take place.
After thirty minutes he got up,
He shook the morning dew off his shiny, silky coat,
He raised his ears - he could hear footsteps.
It was just his imagination.
He strolled a bit further before his nose touched the fence.
He spotted his fat prize.
He crept as quiet as a mouse under the fence.
He leaped towards the chicken.
A puff of feathers flew into the air.
The feathers floated down like snow on Christmas day.
His face was dripping with blood.
He made a quick escape under the fence.
He sprinted off into the woods,
He was a true criminal.
It was the work of a professional.
But the guilt will live with him forever.

Gregory Crabb (12)
St Nicholas School

THE HELICOPTER

The silence is deafening
in the quiet of the night.
In the distance the gentle drone draws nearer and nearer.
The big lights start to shimmer in the mist of the night,
bringing a strange glow to the night sky.
Suddenly the night turns into daylight;
with a huge rage of rumbles,
the leaves begin to tumble.
Down to the ground they fall,
twirling, swirling and whirling
downwards until they meet the forest floor.
As the helicopter swoops
and turns back into the sky
over the trees, it sweeps
out of sight it leaps.

Hayley Matthews (13)
St Nicholas School

ASSASSIN

Storming through the sky
Searching for its target
Scanning the ground for its prey
Searching around night and day
Not a glimmer not a sound
Sweeping through the cold winter air
Locking on its target ready to kill
Strike!
Not a chance not a hope
The ruined town is left for dead
The sly assassin swoops back to its nest.

Andrew Cherrill (13)
St Nicholas School

A Typical Day At School

I rushed into school at a quarter to nine
Sped into the classroom just in time
Register was taken all were in
Hurry to lessons, they're about to begin.

Double science at first
I was five minutes late
Two demerits
Oh isn't this great
I've forgotten my homework, help I'm dead
I wish I had stayed in bed instead.

At lunch-time my friends are having a row
Nobody is speaking, what happens now?
It's pouring with rain
I am all alone
What a disastrous day
I want to go home!

I am watching the time
The clock must have stopped
Maths lasts forever
Hurry up four o'clock

At last the wonderful sound of the bell
I make for the lockers
I am released from hell
Jump into the car, 'Hello Mum
Get me home, that was not fun!'

Hannah Barry (13)
St Nicholas School

LOST AND FOUND

I was on my bed watching the telly
When I heard the front door slam,
Then my sister stormed in, threw my remote
In the bin,
And sat on my bed with a wham.

'I've lost it, I've lost it,' she shouted
'It's very important to me.'
'Lost what?' I replied, 'I can't remember,' she cried
'But it's something beginning with P.

'Your passport maybe,' I suggested,
'A pot, or even a pie,'
'A parcel,' I said, but she shook her poor head,
'It's none of those,' she said with a sigh.

'A parrot maybe,' I said
'A plane or even a pipe,
A purple pansy, or a pig called Dansy
Or a polite little pig of some type.'

Then suddenly her scowl vanishes,
'I remember!' she cried with a shout,
'It's my patience, you punk,' when my heart had sunk,
As she punched both my eyes and walked out.

Jessica Atkins (12)
St Nicholas School

Lost And Found . . .

I was writing a letter to my aunt,
When mother walked into the hot room,
With a big huff and a puff,
With a face full of sorrow and gloom.

'I've lost it, I've lost it,' she said,
'Lost what?' I replied,
'I've forgotten it,' she sighed,
'It's important to me,
But it's something beginning with C.'

'Could it be a carrot,
Or a calf or even your cot,
Or some chocolate, maybe your cake
I know, it has to be your *cat*.'

But mum looked totally blank,
'Well how about a chop,' I said, 'or a chipmunk,
Or a chimpanzee or a cup,
Maybe the chips, or even your mop.'

Suddenly mum shrieked and said, 'Now I remember,'
She started marching towards me like a thunder,
'Of course, your *careless son,* me!'
She screamed and said, '*Yes* it's you and your *cars,'*
She boxed me on my ears and I saw *stars!*

Archchana Radhakrishnan (12)
St Nicholas School

UNTITLED

Out of the soft, calming sky
a bird emerges from a distance.
Swiftly swooping, glides and
dives gracefully.
Zooming and hovering
his wings stretched as they
help him float through the air.
So peaceful.
Fierce and strong, alert and
listening at all times.
Suddenly a crackle in the
bushes beneath him.
Threatening as he is, he darts
towards the bushes, then all that
is left is the shriek and screams
of the prey fading until there
is a silence.

Lauren Harris (13)
St Nicholas School

MY RABBIT

I opened the hutch door;
He was sitting there motionless.
His little damp nose twitched up and down.
He saw the door left open, and ran straight out.
Off he went, kicking his legs up in the air.
He comes to a stop.
His little tiny whiskers twitter in the wind.
His black, silky ears bob up and down.
He creeps behind the shed, not making a sound.
His little tiny head pops round the corner to check
no danger is lurking in the air.

Soon it becomes dark.
The rabbit hops back into his hutch.
He stretches his legs out and falls asleep
after his tiring day in the garden.
I close the hutch door and check it's locked up.
Then I go inside for the rest of the night.

Katie Furlong (12)
St Nicholas School

Freedom

Freedom is when you walk the open road
no one to hold you back

Freedom is when you stare up at the stars
while the world carries on turning

Freedom is when you can take it slowly,
take it at your own pace,
isolated.

Freedom is not when you are stuck in a room
a room full of books
but your destiny's to be free

Life is short.
Life flows fast.

Be free as a dove.

Carlene Banister (14)
St Nicholas School

FREEDOM

Freedom is not
Looking down an endless corridor
past claustrophobic cells
to death row.

Freedom is not
Looking through the crown of thorns
that weave barbed wire boundaries
around a concentration camp

Freedom is not
Looking at the night sky
from the restraining manacles
of a gamekeeper's snare

Freedom is not
Looking in the mirror
seeking reassuring comfort
and finding a stranger

Freedom is not
Looking for the truth
embedded in a spider's web
of lies and deceit

Freedom is
The lifting of a latch
or the turning of a key
or a captured moment
of unfettered liberty.

Sarah Naylor (12)
St Nicholas School

THE SURVIVOR

The hungry slim figure approached the herd quietly.
It had sun-dried grass coloured fur and moved very slowly.
I knew it was a lioness waiting to pounce.
But she was very patient and hid in the grass until the time was right.
She crawled towards her prey licking her lips, deciding which one to have.
The herd carried on grazing unaware of the danger.
But the wind changed and all at once the herd ran away,
leaving just one behind.
The poor thing seemed puzzled, not knowing what to do.
It was the lioness's chance and she pounced.
The prey ran, the lioness chased.
The prey jumped, the lioness grabbed.
There was a short struggle, but against all odds,
the prey ran away and the lioness stopped to rest.
She would not eat that day.

Natalie Polaine (13)
St Nicholas School

FIGHTER JET

Get in for take-off,
Checks and open wings to fly,
Start moving and off you go,
Climbing fast,
Brown and black in the sky,
Glides through the air,
Swoosh,
Going past fast,
Gliding quietly,
Target sighted.
Stay in sight,
Special smokes come out,
As the roar screams.
Prey dead and ready to come home,
For a soft two-footed landing.

David Brierley (13)
St Nicholas School

Buzz

Out of the long silence grows
a buzzing, a constant drone.
Suddenly escaped from the
cocoon of the winter resting
place, it's free.
The bright and beautiful colours
reflected from the sun
of the once sleeping slave.
Starting its journey through the
garden
it starts to ravenously suck up
the grass as though it was
sucking the sweetest nectar
from the finest flower.
Side to side hovering
dangerously into the twilight
eventually finding its way
home, to sleep once more
and to be recognised, for the
duty set, is now complete.

Bobby Ghadami (13)
St Nicholas School

STORM

Shriek like a storm
flowing throughout the night
comes the immense, colossal sound
like a hurricane.
It thunders through the night,
in the dead of night.
Booming headlights,
Camouflaging its dark grey surface,
not caring what's in its way.
A distinct shudder like a hurricane,
Fast, faster, faster,
Roars with a distinct, immense scream
from the monstrous, mighty, machine.
The fumes choke the air,
The lorry is like an elephant.

Emilie Bedford (13)
St Nicholas School

TRUE LOVE

Love is an emotion from the heart,
Which will never keep us apart,
No matter what we'll be together,
You and I forever and ever,

Break up, they want us to,
Leave you I could never do,
You mean the world to me,
I love you, can't you see.

Amy Webb (13)
Shoeburyness County High School

SPEECHLESS

As moonlight fell across the ocean
The ocean was a mirror
Waiting to be shattered
The sound was a silence
Waiting to be broken
A ripple was made
And the mirror was shattered
A dolphin leaped
As if it waited
To break the mirror
And another leaped
It spun with great elegance
The sight was magnificent
The ripples of water
Trickled onto the shore
The silence has now been broken
By the splashes of dolphins leaping
The sounds seemed calming
A distant echoing could be heard
As the dolphins swam away
Every day life now seemed ordinary
Could anything have the same feeling?
I now felt that I was humbled by their presence.

Jodie Abraham (13)
Shoeburyness County High School

DARKNESS

Darkness is the black,
That haunts you at night.
Don't be afraid,
Turn on the light.
You're blinded by it,
It's a bit too bright.
Adjust your eyes,
You'll gain your sight.
Now you're not scared,
You can sit there despite.
The fact that,
You might have got a fright.
You're in your room,
Sitting there at night.
You're not scared,
Because you turned on the light.

Christine Adams (13)
Shoeburyness County High School

SPELLBOUND

I watched my breath fade into the air,
Wondering why I still had to live,
When all that happened was bad,
In my mind was a line between existing and living,
I had crossed it, pushing it aside like all my feelings.

Worries left me and floated away, too long had I let it control my soul
Time is eternal for those who hesitate, but goes too quickly for impatience,
I was trapped in a middle ground,
No sanctuary or peace to be found,
Stuck in existence unable to live.

Spellbound by agony and pain,
That just won't fall like the daily rain,
Renewed by a face that haunted every dream,
Spellbound by love, and blinding tears.

Never able to escape my fears,
A fear of an empty life, with no one by my side,
Unable to get away from it, and swallow my jealous pride,
If I do feel for anyone else, I think it is a sin.
It always ends in tears, nothing compares to him.

Nicola Wood (14)
Shoeburyness County High School

WITCHES

Witches are as ugly as hell,
As I should know.
I was walking along on my own,
Then these three witches sprung me from behind,
I jumped, I screamed, I yelled and yelled,
They cackled and laughed,
I was so scared.
Everything went blank,
Then when I woke up
I turned around and this old hag was staring at me,
When I looked, there were three,
They started to sing,
In croaky old voices,
One grabbed me and started to shake my arm,
I started to kick,
Then all three took me
They lay me down.
This was the end for me,
Aghhhhhhhhhhhhh!

Sarah Haines (12)
Shoeburyness County High School

War Poppies

Bullets flying overhead,
I couldn't take the pain,
Boom, boom and bang,
Were running through my brain.

Each time I looked about,
The battleground looked like blood,
For every rotting body,
Was being trod into the mud.

A pain shot through my body,
Like, knives twisting in my heart,
I knew that I was dying,
I knew from the start.

Spellbound with fear,
I crawled to hide,
From the falling, withering men,
That were dying for their country's pride.

The pain of the bullet,
Was making me see red,
In a couple of hours,
Surely I'll be dead.

I saw my family crying,
I saw my grave full of tears,
A single poppy planted,
That had survived throughout the years.

I'm going to be a poppy,
That survived where dead men fell,
I'm going to touch the gates of heaven,
And not ring the bell.

Spellbound with courage,
I rose onto my feet,
I grabbed my gun and withering friends,
Each of my feet moving with the heartbeat.

Thank you to the poppy,
That was like my leaning tower,
That gave me my will to live,
That gave me my inner power.

Gemma McNevin (15)
Shoeburyness County High School

The Witch And The Wizard

Witches and warlocks fight, they've never fought before,
but I know they did last night,
'cause I was standing on the moor.

The witch said 'Toad' and the wizard turned into one,
The wizard said 'Frog' and the witch turned into one.
Snake, elephant, spider, lizard,
with all the spells that caused a blizzard.

A spell here and a spell over there
all those spells caused quite a scare.

Until one day the wizard said,
'Let's stop these spells I'm almost dead
I've used up all my magic on the witch standing there,
and all I can turn into is a measly brown bear.'

'Alright' said the witch 'I'll stop my spells'
but the sneaky wizard waved his wand,
and sent the witch into the pond.

Now she's wet, a soggy hag,
the wizard's tricks were quite a gag.

Vickie Dann (12)
Shoeburyness County High School

Could This Really Be Love?

As I walk past you once again,
I feel my heart begin to flutter.
The words I want to feel and say,
Nothing comes out but a mere splutter.
As our eyes come to meet,
I feel the blood running through my body,
From my head to my feet.
Your eyes are like crystals,
As blue as the ocean.
Every move you make,
My heart fills with emotion.
When you slowly walk away,
I know that deep in your heart,
You really want to stay.

Jenny Wilson (13)
Shoeburyness County High School

Witches

I swear I saw a witch one night,
Flying high in the sky,
Her broomstick glided through clouds and mist,
I'm not quite sure if she did exist.
My friends make up stories about this witch and
Always tell them with a twitch.
My dad says Satan is her black cat,
And there he sits in her hat,
What have we for tea today, did black cat,
Satan say.
An eye of newt, leg of toad,
In the cauldron here it goes.

Lena Drew (12)
Shoeburyness County High School

SILENCE

Silence as our eyes met.
My heart started to thump
And I saw goose bumps
creeping up my arm.
But I knew with him I
never come to harm.
As our bodies passed
he felt like silk.
His aftershave so strong.
It still lives on.
But in a blink of an eye
he has gone.
Will I see him once again
or am I wrong.

Sophie O'Donoghue (13)
Shoeburyness County High School

THE TRUTH ABOUT ENGLISH TEACHERS

Slimy teachers in disguises, flying over the moon when the sun rises
Plotting plans brewing spells, make children feel not so good
Eating worms, eating snails, cackling away as another child wails
Lying about every grade you get, putting you down another set.
Listening to every sound you make, giving you nightmares until
you wake.
Barking dogs, eating hogs, keeping pets their breeds are pogs.
Odd socks, snaky hair, did you know they never wash their hair.
Understanding the teacher's words, is impossible unless you're a nerd.
Noses tidy, faces neat, change the broomstick into a seat.
Different clothes they have to wear, changing clothes going up the stairs

Matthew Leggett (12)
Shoeburyness County High School

When The Witches Came

Where are the witches, where are the wizards
Where are the ones who blow up the blizzards
They are the ones and here they come
Bubbling up tricks with spells to be done.
No one knows where they come from
No one can guess
No one dares to follow them back where they rest.
The tricks which they've started, the tricks which they've done
Some of them nasty, some are for fun
The things which they have put into
Their very old pot.
The sounds which come out, like crackley, pop
The witches have vanished, the witches have gone
The witches have finished, what they had begun.

Tom Hatley (12)
Shoeburyness County High School

A Fat Black Cat

Once I found a black witch's hat.
I said 'What's that?'
and out popped a black cat.

It said 'I'm a black magical cat,
although I might seem to be very fat.'

'Pick up my hat and I'll take you back,
to where I became very fat.'

With a giggle and a twizzle,
he took me back,
back in the old black hat.

Elisha Ross (13)
Shoeburyness County High School

Bubbling Pot

Through the valley,
Over the hill,
I hear the cackles from the witch,
Her crude spells rhyme,
The smoke from her cauldron fills the air,
It smells so sour.
She flies on her broomstick,
Everyone hides in their cellars,
They don't know what she's stirring up next.
She goes deeper into the town,
All of the people cry,
The witch is coming to get us,
She snatches a child,
A cat and a dog,
She takes them back,
To her bubbling pot.

Ross Ellis (12)
Shoeburyness County High School

The Spell That Went Wrong

It's bubbling, bubbling in the pot
You know the stuff that makes you grow a lot

Newts, worms and spiders too
It's going to be on me in a minute or two

Wait a minute it's happening now
I'm getting bigger and bigger

Wow, Wow, Wow.

Anthony Davis (12)
Shoeburyness County High School

The Wizard

I am a wizard of all disguise,
I am old and very wise,
I am filled with the greatest power,
I live in an old creepy tower.
I've killed a devil, I've killed a witch,
I've killed the poor, I've killed the rich.
I'm undefeated, I am the best,
I come from the south, east, north and west.
I hold the key to unlock the door,
For eternal life and others more.
The secret ingredients to all my power,
I boil in a pot at the top of my tower.

A baby's skin,
The sharpest pin,
A baby's leg,
An eagle's egg,
A baby's nose,
Its fingers and toes,
But my secret ingredient I cannot tell,
For it comes from a faraway place called
Hell!

Wayne Carter (12)
Shoeburyness County High School

The Magician

The magician named Sinbad
was all alone in his tower.
So he went down to his cellar.

There he found his spell being made
The spell he'd been making for
his nurse and maid.

The spell that had cursed his best
friend Dave.
The spell that had made him strong
so now he had grown tall and his
legs were long.

He studied the pot containing frogs
and dogs.
Then in went a spider followed by
a tiger.
And in went the cider to make the spell
stronger.

Hooray the spell was finished,
Hooray the spell was going thinner.
So come on nurse and maid it's time
for dinner.

Claire Paine (12)
Shoeburyness County High School

ONE NIGHT LONG AGO

In the silence of the night,
There was an almighty light,
That shot through the caves,
And over the graves,
The warlock sat in the open plane,
Saying the words that he found again,
The ground swept open and up rose the fire,
To the warlock's own desire,
Out the devil came,
To wreak his havoc once again,
He started on towards the town,
And everybody he did drown;
In the blood of those before,
As he turned towards the people's door,
To claim another sacrifice
So that he can live tonight,
That night the deaths totalled all,
The creature itself didn't fall,
And in the present you're lucky you know,
No one can summon the beast from below.

Andrew Turner (12)
Shoeburyness County High School

SPELLBOUND

They brew their spells at the crack of dawn.
Adding what they can.

Children's toes, a crocodile's nose.
And all different things like that.

They will catch you and scratch you
And tear you into shreds.

They'll eat you whole from out of bowl,
Of gravy and of bread.

Charlotte Reading (11)
Shoeburyness County High School

SPELLBOUND

You can be spellbound,
by many things.
A beautiful woman,
as she sings.
Or perhaps
by a brand new hat,
or a furry ginger cat.

But spellbound,
is neither right or wrong.
Spellbound,
is what you make it.
Spellbound,
is what you feel.
Spellbound,
is there when you need it.

Melanie Jerrum (14)
Shoeburyness County High School

SPELLBOUND

Spellbound makes me think of weird and spooky things,
Like objects floating by themselves.
And chocolate-flavoured shellfish would be a treat,
Funny things like flying feet.

Magical wizards ugly witches with horrible spells,
Magical words like alacazam.
And a sweet-shop all of my own,
Scary tigers and big dinosaurs,
Spooky ghosts and ghouls.

Magical dust that makes you fly,
High, high in the sky.
Mince pies that turn you into a cat,
Or something horrible like falling off a building and going
Splat.

Glyn Parsons (11)
Shoeburyness County High School

SPELLBOUND

In a faraway forest lives a witch and a wizard,
They're cooking their dinner with frogs and lizards.
A trespassing girl is coming along,
Singing her song all day long.
Out of the lair the witch and wizard come,
Scared of the daylight and heat of the sun,
They grab the girl and take her in,
They put her in their cauldron,
And eat her for their din!

Aaron Osborn (11)
Shoeburyness County High School

SPELLBOUND

Fourteen tired hunting dogs,
coming back from their hunt.
With three depressed hunters
with no food or drink.

Five women standing,
around a blazing fire.
Many squawking birds,
in trees and flying high.

Fluffy snow on the ground,
and icicles on the house.
Snowy hills in the background,
and skaters on the frozen lakes.

A man holding a table,
sees the man and hunting dogs.
A man gathering kindling,
sees the woman on the bridge.

Four churches in the middle,
people skating well.
Fields in the distance,
the frozen waterwheel.

Fifty-nine people,
on the ice and snow.
Fourteen dogs and three hunters,
have they far to go?

Crystal Warrington (11)
Shoeburyness County High School

SPELLBOUND

I was sitting down,
Trying to write a poem,
The poem was to be called Spellbound,
Which I thought was strange,
Spellbound could be thought of,
In many, many different ways,
I had written three poems already,
Which no one seemed to like,
So I am still sitting here,
Spellbound.

I was still sitting there,
When the bell went to finish,
It rang forever and I thought,
I would never write a good poem,
And then an idea entered my head,
To write about me, writing,
So I thought and thought some more,
And I decided this is what to do,
I sat there thinking all day,
Spellbound.

Liam Shaw (14)
Shoeburyness County High School

SPELLBOUND, DURING DREAMS

I dived into my imagination,
The sound of things around me died,
As I walked under the dripping canopy,
I realised what life entailed.

My wish was to stay for eternity,
I became spellbound as I gazed,
Why couldn't everything be so natural?
As natural as time that still passed.

The rain fell slowly,
Just like our lives, each one as important as the next,
Waterfalls appearing everywhere,
Each one ending in a river of stars.

The sky was as black as coal,
The stars were as bright as the sun,
Dragging me into their world I realised,
Dreams are not just thoughts in your mind,
They can come true if you want them to!

Jonathan Watson (14)
Shoeburyness County High School

SPELLBOUND

One day a funny bloke.
Who drunk a can of Coke.
He started to cry.
'Cause he couldn't fly,
Oh, he was totally spellbound.
He thought of hypnotism.
But he wouldn't listen.
He thought of seeing a wizard.
But blew up a great big blizzard.
Oh, he was totally spellbound.
He thought of seeing a witch.
But he was a titch.
He thought of eating Twiglets.
But he swallowed big bits.
Oh, he was totally spellbound.
Oh spellbound he really was.

Richard Choules (11)
Shoeburyness County High School

Enchantment

It's seven o'clock, the night has gone,
The day has broken but no bird song.
Silence hangs like a heavy shroud,
This magic has come from a fallen cloud,
I stare out the window and see the mist.
Touching the lake, a soft gentle kiss,
Fingers reach out to touch the banks,
Trees stand still in orderly ranks.
No movement, no colours, not even a sound,
As the mist reaches down to the once warm ground,
Where are the birds, the people, the creatures?
Where is the landscape, the familiar features?
Hidden from view in this moment of time,
A magical moment, a fairytale rhyme,
The curtain comes down the sun's lost its glow,
The mist tells autumn it's time for her show.

Anna Tansley (14)
Shoeburyness County High School

Spellbound

I was spellbound,
By the sun setting over the horizon,
The breaking of the waves,
And the shimmering of the sea,
Are beautiful to me.

The colours reflected by the horizon,
The white foam, rising to the surface when
The waves break,
And the shivering of the sea,
Are all wonders to me.

Dawn Callowhill (14)
Shoeburyness County High School

SPELLBOUND!

It was my birthday,
My grandma sent me a mythical magical book!
I thought it was a load of junk,
I had one look and it was gone?
I was intrigued, I looked and looked,
But I'm afraid to say, the book was no longer with me.

On the next morning I woke to find, the book squashed right up to my nose!
I had another look inside,
Getting ready for its escape,
Of course, this time, not thinking it was a load of junk,
I heard a shout *'Hey Joe get up you don't want to be late for school!'*
I shoved the book in my bag and went to school.

I got to the dreaded place,
But five minutes late,
My teacher said, *'Detention!'*
I wished and wished,
That she would faint or even better, just *'I quit!'*
And guess what, she did, just that,
I had assembly that morning,
Oh how I hated assembly,
To make it worse it was Tuesday,
Double *English*, double *maths* and *geography!*
Again I wished and wished but this time,
I wished for the boiler to *explode* . . . !

Joe Clements (12)
Shoeburyness County High School

The Witch's Stew

Over a thousand miles I come,
I am a witch but I'm not the only one.
I have made a poisoned stew,
Which is especially for you.
I threw in a cat, I threw in a dog,
I threw in a bat, I threw in a frog,
I threw in a tiger, I threw in a snake,
I threw in a spider, I threw in a rake.
I kidnapped a child from his bed,
I then killed him and chopped off his head.
You don't believe in the kingdom of witches,
So I put in some believing spell pinches.
You don't like us, you think we're mad,
You don't think we're good, you know we're bad.
Hee, hee, hee.

Adam Shuttleworth (13)
Shoeburyness County High School

Spellbound

This is the night when wizards rise,
Magic and sorcery flying through the sky!

This is the night when phantoms hide,
When all the wizards come out in tribes!

This is the night when angels sing,
Nobody knows what luck they'll bring!

This is the night when devils roar,
They've got sorcery, magic and much, much, more!

Adam Salmons (11)
Shoeburyness County High School

SPELLBOUND

I once walked out of my house,
With a tiny funny mouse.
It said let's go under the ground,
To see the wizard spellbound.
I knew he was very nice,
He let us eat all of his ice.
His cave was a crazy place,
It was all made out of lace.
The wizard would not kill a fly,
He wouldn't let anyone die.
He would put a spell on them,
But they might turn into a hen.
Sometimes he would do things wrong,
He kept singing this awful song.
He made the song up on his own,
Because he was always alone.
The song was not very good,
Because his brain was made out of wood.
Someday I would prove,
That his songs and spells would improve.
I really did like that wizard,
But he kept a strange pet lizard.
He also kept a pet bee,
But he taught him not to hurt me.
Spellbound acts just like a clown,
So if I'm with him, I never get down!

Emma Sheehan (11)
Shoeburyness County High School

WITCHES

The witches have made me spellbound
Under their evil witchery
Before they put me under the spell
I heard them shout and yell
'Eye of frog and tongue of dog
Blind bat's wing
Mix it up together like a thick broth'
I felt a cold, bony hand grab me
'Now eat! You miserable little brat'
They've got me spellbound
I felt like a rat
They've got me spellbound
I can't get out
Nowhere to run
Nowhere to go
They've got me spellbound
I'm spellbound
Spellbound

Kylie Jenkins (12)
Shoeburyness County High School

WITCH'S POEM

Every day I walk to school,
I see the witch on her broom.
I wonder why she wants to fly,
Every time I see her in the sky.
I wonder where her cat is,
That's if she's got a cat.
Thinking what she does at home,
That's if she's got a home.

Anthony Crinks (11)
Shoeburyness County High School

THE WITCH, CAMILLA

Camilla the witch was a pretty creature,
Don't trust 'er, don't trust 'er.
With eyes twinkling like stars,
Don't trust 'er, don't trust 'er,
Fair hair and lovely skin,
Don't trust 'er, don't trust 'er,
She's wicked through and through,
Don't trust 'er, don't trust 'er

She walks to the kitchen,
There's trouble brewing, there's trouble brewing,
To where the cauldron lives,
There's trouble brewing, there's trouble brewing.

She's preparing an awful spell,
There's trouble brewing, there's trouble brewing.
It's the dreaded love curse,
There's trouble brewing, there's trouble brewing.

In goes the tiger's heart,
Stir it round, stir it quick
Making sure the contents stay thick.
Next a dash of dragon's liver,
Stir it round, stir it quick,
Making sure the contents stay thick.
Finally added is a few newts' eyes,
Stir it round, stir it quick,
Making sure the contents stay thick.

No man in the land is safe,
Beware, beware,
'Cos once under her spell,
Beware, beware
She'll bleed him dry.

Daniel Rivers (12)
Shoeburyness County High School

THE WITCH

The witch she flew on Hallowe'en
Making children stare and scream
She laughed and swooped through
The sky at night
Her black cat, holding tight.

Her pointed hat, her long, bent nose
Her darkened cape, and jet black clothes
She swoops and dives
Goes round and round
Scaring children on the ground.

She flies around but once a year
Casting spells on those all near
So stay inside or you might
Be a rabbit for *eternity*.

Claire Parish (12)
Shoeburyness County High School

SPELLBOUND

He's the one I truly love,
His eyes are like the stars above.
I've found him at last,
I think I know him from the past.
I think about him night and day,
And never want to go away.
He's there in my heart,
And we never want to depart.
I listen to the beautiful sounds,
He always leaves me spellbound.

Michele Davies (14)
Shoeburyness County High School

They're Coming

Witches alive
Witches dead
Witches scaring people in bed
Children crying
People scared
They're coming, they're coming
So be prepared
They're coming tonight
You're in for a fright
So hold on tight
And leave on the light.
They're old
They're hairy
They're ugly
They're scary
The warts on their noses
Are disgusting, like their toeses
And they will eat you alive
When they arrive
'Cause that's what they are
Witches.

Vicki Wells (12)
Shoeburyness County High School

The Witch

She let out a screech, a cackle, a cry
Evil reflected in her bloodshot eye,
Weaving terror throughout the town,
What secrets she kept in her flowing gown!
Darkness her saviour, her weapon a sword,
Light was her enemy, there was never a lord.

The children she met were transfixed by her stare,
The wart on her nose, her sea-green hair.
She knew nothing of guilt, she felt no remorse
For the fear she drove with her mighty force.
Her aim was to fill your heart with dread.
Hers was of stone and was cased in lead,

So beware of a screech, a cackle, a cry
Run away from the sound
Don't let your soul die!

Jenny Crouch
Shoeburyness County High School

Spellbound

When I think of spellbound
My mind goes beyond belief.
I think of magical things
Like wizards and witches
That drag you to the ground.

I feel involved in mythical
stories and fantasies.
Hearing amazing sounds,
The sounds were bellowing
and getting closer to me.

Alex Cuthbert (11)
Shoeburyness County High School

SPELLBOUND

Smoke was rising from the trees in the woods,
As I ran to look to see what it was.
I saw a little house which looked so bare,
So I looked through the window and began to stare.
I saw a blue light,
Which was shining so bright,
So I peered through the door,
And almost fell to the floor,
Then I tripped up the step,
And fell down a hole,
I ended up somewhere I don't really know,
I followed the light and it led me down to a cellar,
And standing there was a handsome young fellah,
His big blue eyes,
And his blond wavy hair.
Made me want to always stare,
I walked up behind him,
And the blue light was blinding,
Then I took his hand and pulled him away,
He cuddled me and said 'Good day,'
I said 'Hello
But I have to go,
I'll meet your tomorrow,
By the rabbits' burrow.'
Then the next day came,
And I saw him again,
And we fell in love,
Like a pair of turtle doves.

Donna Horner (14)
Shoeburyness County High School

DESTINY

We stood together, hand in hand,
Yet our minds were worlds apart.
But we were kept from falling,
By the flame within her heart.

And when I looked into her eyes,
My heart would skip a beat,
And with hatred all around us,
Our love withstood defeat.

A love so pure and very rare,
Our hearts had surely found,
But even with her by my side,
My mind was still spellbound.

When we looked upon ourselves,
We thought this had to be.
That we were brought together,
At the choice of destiny.

A spellbound mind, to ease the pain,
Of a love that used to be.
A spellbound mind, to place the blame,
Upon that of destiny.

Tommy Dickinson (16)
Shoeburyness County High School

SPELLBOUND

I was walking down the road, quite near my home,
When I was spellbound by something which had never been shown.
It was a super-fast computer with a super-fast Pentium!
It was like something from the next millennium.
It was excellent, it was brill!
It was great, such a thrill!

I was on this game on the third level,
When I heard something like ringing metal.
I blinked my eyes,
And to my surprise,
My computer I could find not a shred,
Because I had awakened in my bed.

Mark Jarvis (12)
Shoeburyness County High School

THE FUNNY SPELLBOUND WITCH

There was a funny witch,
Believe it if you can.
She chuckles funny laughs,
She hangs upside down.
She catches human beings
She cooks their skin and flesh.
She rides on a broomstick.
With Mog, her black cat.
She finds her way around,
With her big green eyes.
Scares everyone away with Faye,
Her loving bat.
Tall dark trees,
Looking over her house.
The tower as tall as a skyscraper,
I saw the witch up there,
I don't know why she wants to stay up there.
Maybe she just wants to make me . . .
Spellbound!

Susan Pleasant (11)
Shoeburyness County High School

SPELLBOUND

Spellbound,
What does it mean?

Does it mean magical,
Enchanted or mythical?
Or does it mean speechless,
Unbelievable,
Or amazed?
Will it leave you shocked,
Entranced,
Or in a daze?

Spellbound,
What does it mean?

Charlotte Smyth (11)
Shoeburyness County High School

SPELLBOUND

You are in your own little world of happiness,
Thinking about the one that you love,
It seems to take over your thoughts and dreams,
As sweet as a pure white dove.

The love for someone is so deep and true,
But still it's so hard for some to say 'I love you,'
You can't sleep, you can't eat, it's always on your mind,
Because a love like that is so hard to find.

His eyes, his hair, his gentle loving touch,
Which you always miss so very much,
You can't wait to see him every day,
It's only love that can make you feel this way.

Joanne White (14)
Shoeburyness County High School

SPELLBOUND

Looking at me from below,
I see his eyes glow,
My heart beats faster,
Then I float away.

Turning everywhere, I seem spellbound,
Do I deserve this?
He doesn't want me, does he?

Is this real love,
Or just a silly phase?
But my love for him will never fade.

People warn me to steer clear,
But I don't care about their fears,
Should I listen to them,
Or stay with him?

Laura Cornwell (13)
Shoeburyness County High School

CAPTIVATED

Every time there's a cloudless night,
We look up to see a wondrous sight.
Flugent, gleaming, baffling burning,
Undiscovered, unfound, shimmering, shining.
Alien, spooky, supernatural, unmapped,
So bizarre, my mind won't adapt.
Superb, vibrant, eerie, radiant,
Weird, obscure, bizarre, fluorescent.
Mythical, magical, marvellous, bright,
Twinkle, twinkle, in the night,
That's what planets and stars are like.

Louise Thomas & Laura Watkins (12)
Shoeburyness County High School

SPELLBOUND

Spellbound is a myth,
Dragons and monsters that's all,
Witches and goblins, wizards and hobbits.
And people that live underground.

In the dark of night,
They come into sight,
From the dark and gloomy,
They come out to me,
As I am the witch of the night.

Spellbound can be love,
Sweet as a dove,
With a boy or a girl,
Transforms you to a passion,
Which makes your mind swirl.

Love is like a potion,
It puts your mind in motion,
Your heart beats fast,
You wish it could last,
At the end of the day,
You gave your heart away
But she had to go away.

Stephen Craven (14)
Shoeburyness County High School

SPELLBOUND

Spellbound over you
The way you look, the way you move
I just can't stop thinking about you

Since you left me, it's never the same
Always wondering why. Could I have made you happier?
There'll never be another you.

We were together for so long
I just want to know what I did wrong
I always loved you, you didn't love me.

Rupert Chappell (14)
Shoeburyness County High School

The Witch's Spell

The cave was dark and damp
And full of dirty, violent bats
At the end, a witch did stand
Waving her bony, cut up hands
Saying her spell and cackling aloud.

Guts of a rabbit, body of a worm
Hoof of a horse, head of a goat
Leg of a sheep, blood of a stoat
Cauldron bubble, bring me a spell
With lots of trouble.

I watched in vain as she
Strained and strained to bring up
A spell which arose from hell
The cave lit a circle of fire
Which as she spoke rose higher and higher.

Eyes of a frog, toe of a toad
Make my spell arise, arise
And stun everyone before their eyes
And then they will see that I'm the one
The witch of the century because I'm the
Greatest one.

Michael Box
Shoeburyness County High School

THE PRINCE AND THE FROG

In the enchanted woods the prince lies low.
He lies in the sun.
All day he sleeps
until he hears a bang from
a little house beyond.

The witch is old and wrinkly
with grey matted hair
and there she stands, making a spell
to frighten people and children.
The prince wakes up and walks,
He stops at the house
She comes out and
Puff!
He's gone
He's a
Frog!

Amy Varney & Jodie Treveil (12)
Shoeburyness County High School

A BROKEN SPELL

Kate fell in love the boy of her dreams,
All she could think about was him,
She'd never let go of a word he'd say,
She'd hold it tight and keep it safe.

Each day the feeling grew stronger,
In every possible way,
She thought about him,
Dreamed about him,
Until the day came.

Kate walked past the bus stop,
Gazing at his face,
He asked her to stop and wait,
And told Kate he loved her to her face.

A spell has been broken,
She was out of a trance,
She could stop dreaming about him,
Because now was her chance.

Rupal Kataria (13)
Shoeburyness County High School

MY LOVE FOR YOU

Our love is so strong,
We can't be separated,
You don't know how my heart aches,
Just to be near you.
I tried for so long,
To find love everlasting,
Was love in all the wrong places?
I'm not the same without you,
I need to be with you,
Put your trust in me,
I'm your best friend.
You can depend on me,
I'll be there when you need me.
You're an angel from heaven,
Here to protect me.
Words can't express my love for you.

Laura Needham (13)
Shoeburyness County High School

SPELLBOUND

As best friends we start,
Getting to know each other well.

How long is this going to last?
Totally under each other's spell.

Talking, walking, eating, drinking,
What is going to happen next?

This is going well, we're thinking,
But what comes after in the text?

Going here and there and everywhere,
Together we go round and round.

Thoughts abound of what to wear,
Until we're both utterly spellbound.

Samantha Bromfield (13)
Shoeburyness County High School

DOLPHINS

Dolphins, dolphins, everywhere I look,
dolphins, dolphins, even in my books,
dolphins, dolphins, even on my bed,
dolphins, dolphins, even on my legs,
dolphins, dolphins, I see them everyday,
dolphins, dolphins they are a bit far away,
dolphins, dolphins, they are really smooth,
dolphins, dolphins, I can hardly move.
dolphins, dolphins, in my dream,
dolphins, dolphins, they're swimming down the stream,
dolphins, dolphins, on my hands,
dolphins, dolphins, even on my hair bands.

Caroline Burwood (11)
Shoeburyness County High School

SPELLBOUND

His long blond hair rests on his shoulders,
His emerald-like eyes look at me,
He smiles so sweet, dimples on either side,
As deep as caves, as soft as sand.

His gentle touch and carrying voice
Covers me with love,
Everyone turns green with envy,
To see him by my side.

His strong Irish accent, so easy to understand,
He jokes and plays with the other lads,
The other members of the band.

Jessica Stackhouse (14)
Shoeburyness County High School

TRAPPED IN LOVE

In a world of my own
I feel so alone.
I'm just holding on
To something so far gone.

I see you pass by
I wish it was you and I.
My feelings inside
Make me want to hide.

When will this feeling cease
Will I ever find peace?
They say time heals
I will see what it reveals.

Beth Spreadborough (13)
Shoeburyness County High School

SPELLBOUND

His shiny brown eyes
Caught my eye
His short brown hair made me want to stare
He glanced at me
We fell in love
All I could see was turtle doves
He began to walk over
My heart began to pound
My knees turned to jelly
I couldn't hear a sound
He stood in front of me
And said 'Hello,
What's your name?' he said
'Wouldn't you like to know?'
I told him my name
He took my hand
It felt like he led me to a faraway land
He held me in his arms
I knew it was love
Like a dove asleep
With a pillow of love
Could it be true,
Or was it a dream?
I didn't really care
It felt true to me.

Tracey Whitbread (13)
Shoeburyness County High School

Spellbound

On the wind, the warlock glides,
Moaning love songs to his bride.
Cackling witch calls in reply,
Swiftly soars, together they fly.

Through branches lit by moonlight bright,
On magic 'All Hallows Eve' night.
Twisting, twirling through the air,
They rise in unison, this pair.

Now together evil work,
You never know where they may lurk.
As dawn appears, they fly away,
Shunning the sunlight of the day.

Through the flowers, fairies tiptoe,
Plants respond, thrive well and grow.
Dancing in a fiery ring,
Marking grasses while they sing.

Vibrant colours, wings ablaze,
Shimmering in the morning's haze.
Banishing all dread and fear,
Love abiding, guardians dear.

All are safe, witches gone,
Evils abolished one by one.
Children playing, hear their call,
Cloak of protection over all.

Stuart Norris (13)
Shoeburyness County High School

SPELLBOUND

His dark brown shining eyes looked at me,
And I went all funny at the knees,
His shades so cool,
And a smile so sweet,
He smells so good,
And that makes me weak.

The gentle cuddle of his gorgeous hands,
And a personality that is so sweet,
The funny words he says to me,
Make me laugh and make me weep.

The beautiful rose he passes to me,
Represents love and harmony,
He sings a song so peacefully,
That I fall asleep.

Natalie Munro (13)
Shoeburyness County High School

SPELLBOUND

When you are spellbound,
Does it feel like magic running through you?
Do you feel enthralled?
Or is it just a feeling you get?

Is it really something, or is it beyond belief?
Is it a mythical story, or is it really there?
Does it make you fascinated?
Or does it seem weird?

Do you feel captivated or is it really abnormal?
I think that I would be all those things and more!

Helen Barnecutt (11)
Shoeburyness County High School

CAPTURED

I cast my fly
Onto the still water,
Slowly it sinks into the murky depths.
Will the fish come?
I don't know;
Wait, patiently.
A smooth creature glides towards the fly.
Smooth, shiny lips open . . .
Oranges, blues and yellows disappear.
I slowly draw the trout,
Closer and closer to the bank.
My captive struggles; then lies limp.
Bright pattern fades. I change my mind.
Trout slowly slithers through my hands,
Free to be alone, again.

Ben Sandford (13)
Shoeburyness County High School

SPELLBOUND

S pellbound really is an interesting world,
P robably one of the most magical,
E ntranced, enthralled and all words like that.
L et spellbound sound like a magic ball,
L ime green, red and all of these colours.
B ring balls, books with these wonderful covers,
O ctagons, pentagons and all shapes like that,
U ndo the power of *Spellbound* with a snap!
N ever ever is the spell going to be broken.
D odge it! Miss it! Do whatever you can because if you get hit,
 you will know what I mean!

James Jones (11)
Shoeburyness County High School

A Little Dragon

I had a little dragon
Nothing it would do
I searched in all the playgrounds
For something it could chew

'Oh little boy,' I begged
'I have a little dragon
Nothing it will do,
The little boy looked up at me and said
'Take him to the zoo.'

I have a little dragon
Nothing it will do
Will you please come and play
As he mopes around all day?

Grant Bailey (12)
Shoeburyness County High School

Spellbound

I was spellbound,
The blinding, auburn sun shone and hit my eyes.
As it rose over the apple green hills
The cold, sharp morning air hit my face
I came over in a tingly chill.
As the sun climbed up over the tree tops
it climbed on to my face.
A warm tingle rushed down my spine.
I had never experienced anything so pure
and beautiful before in my life.
If only it had never ended that
one cold morning, early in spring.

Gregory Crowhurst (14)
Shoeburyness County High School

SPELLBOUND

Spellbound could mean anything,
It doesn't bother me.
It could mean good luck or bad luck,
I don't really care, you see.

Wizards, sorcerers and witches too,
Better watch out,
Or they'll come after you!

Cast a spell,
Turn me into a frog.
Put a curse on me,
Then surround me with fog.

In the cauldron,
The water bubbles,
Then suddenly a wart-faced witch appears,
Double trouble!

I don't really care,
It doesn't bother me,
The word spellbound,
Could mean anything, you see!

Claire Allen (13)
Shoeburyness County High School

Hypnotist

There is a word that springs to mind
when people seem so very kind
we see it on the TV shows
how people can get high and low
a click of a finger, an intense delight
in a sleepy or dreamy kind of might

For the audience an amusing sight,
the volunteers look straight through the light
dazzled by the way they act
although unusual, this is the fact
doing things they wouldn't do
unaware of what they are going through.

This word is the hypnotist
he can have you under by the flick of the wrist
saying words that calm you down
and at anytime can bring you round
so when they hear that familiar sound
back to normal, not spellbound.

Julie Smith (17)
Shoeburyness County High School

The Witch's Brew

Hubble bubble, toil and trouble
I am making a witch's brew using an eye of a toad and
a head of a snake,
Some evil words, all directed at you.
I stir with my stick in order to make the wickedest evil
spell in all the land
and all made by my own wrinkly hand.

Matthew Wells (12)
Shoeburyness County High School

SPELLBOUND

Lying unconscious in a bed,
Hearing voices in my head,
Seeing misty clouds,
In the sky, in my mind's eye.

I know not how I got in this state,
Help! I need to be able to relate,
How did I arrive?
Spellbound,
Trance-like, can't relate.

Flying from here to there,
My mind is in a Whirl,
Hearing squishing, squelching noises,
My mind's in a complete turmoil.

I hear a man start to talk
'Tell me about your problems, Mark.'

I start to talk,
I know not what I say,
It seems like a familiar play,
Have I watched too much *Casualty*?
I wonder as I lay.

Squishing, squelching noises,
Are not so muffled now,
A man says, 'On the count of three
I wish to release you from *Spellbound,*
One;
Two;
Three.'

Jenny Haysom (14)
Shoeburyness County High School

Alien Spellbound

Spellbound by the things I saw,
Hoping they could show me more,
Who do they want,
Me or you?
But now I am here,
What shall I do?

I'm in the sky high above,
Like a bewildered flying dove,
Get me down,
From this floating place,
Get me back,
With the human race.

As I floated back to earth
Wondering what all this was worth,
I realised that,
They weren't so bad
They were only,
Alone and sad

Chris Stanford (14)
Shoeburyness County High School

Spellbound

After taking these magical potions,
You can't dabble with your emotions.
You're under a spell of love,
You're flying in the air like a silver dove.

Feelings captured in your soul,
As time goes by you lose control.
Counting every second apart,
Run to greet him with a soaring heart.

You're under the tranquil moonlight in a trance,
He's holding you tightly as you dance.
Gorgeous brown eyes full of affection,
Dancing slowly, you hold him for protection.

Drawing you nearer, your knees feel weak,
He bends down and kisses you tenderly on the cheek,
You kiss him passionately, your love so strong,
You'll always be in his heart where you belong.

Henrietta Ross (13)
Shoeburyness County High School

TRAPPED IN A LOVE SPELL

A spell was cast,
over me just yesterday.
And now I'm trapped in a,
Love spell.
Every time I see him,
I get a cold shiver down my back.
I dream all day.
I don't pay attention.
I can't concentrate on,
anything.
He's like a strawberry
sweet and pure.
I think of him day,
and night, he's always on
my mind.
The clock struck 3,
and *puff,* the spell was broken.

Linzi Tegerdine (12)
Shoeburyness County High School

GHOSTS

Ghosts have always interested me.
I've never seen or heard one creeping
about though.
I like to be scared that's probably
why I like them.
Ghosts can be mean or nasty.
Kind or friendly.
I wouldn't mind being a ghost.
Jump through walls, play lots
of tricks.
There could be ghosts in the attic,
The downstairs cupboard and
even the garden shed.
At night they probably come alive
and during the day, they go back
to their graves.
I'd love to be able to meet a ghost.
But I bet I'll never get the chance.

Natasha Monerville (11)
Shoeburyness County High School

SPELLBOUND

'Joey, Joey . . . ' his teacher shouted out,
Just before she had any doubts,
But Joey wasn't listening,
Joey didn't shout,
Joey was spellbound by the clout,
That the boy in the playground got,
After all he was a pain,
And Joey wished he'd got the cane.

Adam Mack (14)
Shoeburyness County High School

SPELLBOUND

In goes frogs' legs
Newts' eyes too
In goes anything
Just to poison you

Dogs' eyes
Cats' tails
Anything to hand
I'm out to kill you
Don't you understand

You'd better run for cover
You'd better run and hide
Because when I catch you
You are going to die

Tina Wagstaff (15)
Shoeburyness County High School

CHRISTMAS

Christmas, Christmas, my favourite thing
out of anything.
It takes me up to space, lots of presents to open
and lots of things to do.
I hate it when it goes away. The Christmas tree
looks pretty with all the decorations up on the walls,
Lots of Christmas cards to write,
That's all I think about,
Christmas make me happy,
It brings my family closer together,
This is what is called spellbound.

Rebecca Acklam (11)
Shoeburyness County High School

THE WITCH

I saw a witch on a broomstick
last night, flying in the sky.
Big and round and short and fat,
not a pleasant sight,
She looked at me whilst flying high
and flew down from the dark night sky.
She stared at me and gave a gleam,
I thought that was strange, as I thought
she'd be mean.
I smiled at her and she seemed to be
the nicest witch I'd ever seen.
She got on her broomstick and flew away,
But I still remember that witch to this day.

Samantha Treveil (12)
Shoeburyness County High School

SPELLBOUND

3 days to Christmas
Nearly here
I can't wait any longer
2 days to Christmas
It is Christmas eve tomorrow
Go carol singing
Just 1½ days left
1 day to Christmas
We are going to a party
0 days to Christmas

Christmas is here!

Sam Dawson (11)
Shoeburyness County High School

SPIDERS ARE SPELLBOUND

Like a tightrope walker,
Thirty foot high,
His arms spread so wide
Ready to fly.
The spider's evil eyes,
Burning up like a fire,
The transparent body, clear as glass,
Send shivers up your spine.
The web is a warning of danger.
Long legs like a stilt walker
Mouth turned round the opposite way,
To give the sense of horror. Trees covered in webs,
Sparkling like a jewel
Webs as thin as cotton,
Spider, ready to die.

Ruth Wareham (14)
Shoeburyness County High School

SPELLBOUND (LOVE)

Love is your smile,
Love is the stars in your eyes,
Love is what you mean to me,
Love is to be happy just like me.

Love is the way you look at me,
Love is the way your lips touch mine,
Love is the way we walk hand in hand,
Love is the way you make me laugh,
Love is the way you make me cry,
Love is the way you make me feel.

Donna Rennell (13)
Shoeburyness County High School

SPELLBOUND

A witch's spell goes like this,
Frogs' heads,
Newts' legs,
Part of a cat's tail,
Two cows' eyes
And three dead flies.

In they all go,
they must mix,
anyone who drinks this,
will surely be bewitched.

Witches here,
witches there,
all dancing and chanting,
everywhere.

Amanda Wilkinson (14)
Shoeburyness County High School

THE WITCH IN BLUE

I went to sleep one night,
A witch came up to my house
And gave me a fright.
My bed bugs dared not bite
And the whole room set alight with fright.

The witch came in blue
And it cast a spell on me.
I was terrified so much so,
I woke in a start
To find myself staring at
A picture on the wall of the witch in blue.

Adrian Woolner (13)
Shoeburyness County High School

THE LITTLE DEVIL SPELL

My little brother and I
Were all alone in the house one night
He gave me such
A fright that night
I did not know
What to say

He turned into a little devil
And made an evil spell
He turned me into
A frog that night
The spell soon broke
When my mum came in
And that was the end
Of the evil spell.

Amy Barns (11)
Shoeburyness County High School

SWEET REVENGE!

The figure in black seen through the trees,
hidden by a veil of leaves.
Dancing round the cauldron pot,
waiting for it to become hot.

'In goes an ear of dog
a hair of horse,
an adder's tongue,
a fish's gill
together in the pot they *kill!'*

Bubble, bubble the pot's red hot,
time to get out the lot!

Alison Lindsay (13)
Shoeburyness County High School

SPELLBOUND

I love hamsters because they're intelligent.

Loveable is the word for hamsters,
On the wheel they go,
Vets help hamsters,
Eating will keep them alive.

Home is where hamsters belong,
All hamsters are soft and cuddly,
Make a bed for them,
Step aside, let them run around,
They need our love,
Eating more, will make them fat,
Rest them a lot,
Sweet, is what a hamster is.

Kerry Malone (11)
Shoeburyness County High School

SPELLBOUND

I had a friend,
My best friend, indeed.
I trusted her,
She trusted me.
The more and more I trusted her,
The more and more she controlled me.
I couldn't control myself,
She kept controlling me.
In my mind,
People helped me through this.
People were there for me,
Now she is out,
Now I can get on with my life!

Lynette Rees (13)
Shoeburyness County High School

Spellbound

Captivated and enthralled as I watch in
admiration,
So much strength, power and skill,
it's enthralling to see.
The fascination is hard to describe,
As I sit mesmerised, dreaming of being able to play in
such a transfixed and captivating way.
I'm under a spell, I'm hooked, I'm gripped,
There's nothing else like the feeling I get,
When I watch, when I play, it's my,
Inspiration it's my every day *'Netball'*
I'm spellbound in every way.
I'm entranced I'm possessed but to me
It's just the best, nothing else gives me
Such a buzz *'nothing'* not the way
Netball does!

Kate Day (15)
Shoeburyness County High School

Addiction

Control over body and soul,
Never being able to let go.
Transfixed upon the colour gold,
Running through the heart and soul.
Your fingers reaching, reaching as far as they will go,
Never, never being able to let go.
The clock strikes going on and on, like my mind,
Whining, whining going round and round.
Why won't someone help me let *go.*

Sarah Hulbert (13)
Shoeburyness County High School

SPELLBOUND

I'm running as fast as I can,
The witch is coming nearer and nearer
to catch me.
When she does she locks me up in a cage,
But every time she does that,
I somehow escape from her.
But every time I escape,
She catches me again,
and everything goes all over again and again.

But one day when she caught me,
She locked me up inside a wall
That she made with her own spell.
I knew then something was wrong,
I tried to escape but it was no good,
It wasn't like the cage.
But suddenly in a weird, scary voice,
It said 'You'll never escape from here,
You'll die like the others.
I wondered where the voice came from,
But I couldn't find out.
I knew then I'll die like the others,
and there was no way I could escape.

Rohee Khalique (11)
Shoeburyness County High School

Spellbound

Spellbound as I could cope
As I was walking down Main Street with high hope
What was my problem, I don't know
'Cause I was spellbound as I do show

A man was shouting in the distance
A dog was barking with resistance
A car was honking its alarm
A horse was neighing in its barn
But I didn't hear that noisy lot
Because I was stuck like a baby in its cot
Spellbound as I could be
What was the reason?
You tell me!

Looking up at the moon
Looking round for any clue
Is it me or is it you?
Please help me I need to know too
Lost in my thoughts, my mind is untouched
Why am I spellbound this much?

Spellbound, spellbound what does it mean?
Surprised, scared oh in my dreams
Maybe it's bemused, transfixed or charmed
Could be something that makes you alarmed!

Amy Sullivan (13)
Shoeburyness County High School

Spellbound

The old witches sitting in the dark smoky room,
Boiling the spell in a pan from the book.
The eerie lights making their faces scary,
Gleaming teeth that are stained.
Waiting for little children to come out and play,
When the clock strikes they all go out.
Then when they come back all of a sudden,
They are *spellbound.*

When the bubble comes in the pan,
It's too hot get the fan.
Stirring with the spoon, it's too misty in the room,
Making you feel really dizzy that's because it's really fizzy.
Then all of a sudden you have found,
That you are really *spellbound.*

Charlotte Dersley (13)
Shoeburyness County High School

Witches

Never look at witches during the night,
Otherwise you will get a very big fright.
They cackle when they laugh,
They cut their victims in half,
The nose on their faces are a nasty sight.

The poor witches ride on brooms,
The rich ones ride on vacuums.
They cast evil spells,
And have horrible smells,
And send the kids in a room with the fumes.

Michelle De-Pass (13)
Shoeburyness County High School

THE CAVE

An empty cave gives a bright glow
We enter to see what it is
A cauldron burning fiery red
A spell must be inside it
Further and further
Deeper and deeper
Into the cave I go
With shelves of weird and horrible things
Of nasty, of wonderful things
I wonder who lives here

The blood of a toad
I bet it isn't
The tooth of a bat
I tell you it's not
The mould of a mole
You can see it in the name
A horse's hoof
The tail of a rabbit
They're supposed to be lucky not bad
It's probably a real big hoax

From a dark cave
We come to the entrance
We see lots of people standing outside
Or is it just one person?
It has a pointed hat
It also has a very long stick
Which looks like a broom
It's coming nearer or are we going closer
A horrible face becomes clearer
A flash and . . .

Mark Delf (12)
Shoeburyness County High School

THE MYSTIC WITCH

A mystic witch and a cast spell
And under this spell I fell.
I became confused and dazed
And more amused and even amazed.

This spell put me in a golden trance
I'm spinning like a wild dance,
And whilst twizzling round and round
I realised I'd become spellbound.

I needed to get out of this spell today
So I planned to send the witch away.
I grabbed her shiny long black cape
So that I could make a quick escape.

This weird witch that I'd feared
Suddenly had disappeared.
I looked back to see where the witch would be
She was nowhere near which made me *free.*

Katherine Ball (12)
Shoeburyness County High School

WITCHES

In the woods beside a tree,
There is a little witch that looks at me.
So I stare and I stare but I can't figure out
Who it could be.
So I sit down and I think
But there is something
I just can't see.

Kelly Bowers (12)
Shoeburyness County High School

Witch Ways

As I walk down the street the trees stand still
The air is still holding a mystic chill.
The mist lies like layers gently moving around
The spiders' webs reaching down to the ground.
A chill runs down the base of my spine
A figure emerges in the space of time.
Nearer and nearer the figure approaches
The distant sound of horses and coaches.
I cannot move, I cannot run
Stuck to the ground like chewing gum.
A hand reaches out and grabs my wrist
It pulls me along deep into the mist.
Into a cavern as black as night
No hope now no one in sight.
Inside the air is thick and musty
The walls are damp the ground all dusty.
In the centre points a finger of light
The moon shining through as hard as it might.
I'm in a cage surrounded by bats
Screeching and crying ignored by their cats.
Three witches sit and cackle with glee
Pointing their fingers and staring at me.
A cauldron hangs low over a fire
The hags start chanting a terrible choir.
In goes beetles, spiders and fleas
Frogs' legs, nettles, ant eggs and *me*.
The chanting gets louder I'm starting to shake
A voice shouts out 'Emma are you awake.'
It's only a dream it's not really true
At least I don't think so . . . how about you?

Emma Tansley (12)
Shoeburyness County High School

The Little Old Men

As the evening draws in,
I see little old men
Go into the dark,
Then I hear a dog bark.

I go to bed
And look out of my window,
A flash of green,
A flash of red,
Whizzing round my head.

I walk out in the night
And have a fright,
A big black cauldron,
With little wizards saying,

A tail of a cat,
A bark of a dog,
The toe of a frog,
The eye of a newt.

Walking round and throwing things in,
Then the little old men start to sing.

Then they see me standing there,
And start to chase me naked and bare,
Then they all just disappear.

So I go back to bed
And wish to see them all again.

Kelly Wall (12)
Shoeburyness County High School

The Scary Witches

Thunder and lightning in the sky,
Witches come in with a blind eye.
In they go to cast a spell,
Enough to blow you into Hell.
All the children running around,
Worrying about the witches spellbound.

All the witches in ragged clothes,
Walking around the black old cauldron.
Knobbly knees and hairy legs,
Old shaky bodies,
With hardly any hair.

Witches are terrible,
Old terrifying looking things.
They wait to catch a child,
To help them make a spell.
That spell is the most unpleasant one,
The one that we all hate.
That unpleasant spell is called,
'Spellbound'

Daniella Tullio (13)
Shoeburyness County High School

The Magic Window

The magic window is an ordinary looking window
The window is only magic when you think hard
When you look in it you see shiny lights
and a bonfire in the middle of trees
with lights flashing
and the face of a witch.

Vicky Whitehair (12)
Shoeburyness County High School

COMPUTERS

I walked down the street and I looked in the shop,
What I saw in the window made me hop.
It was a brand new computer with all the latest stuff,
My old computer's good but that's not enough!

My old computer has got 16 MB RAM,
But this one's even got dram!
My computer's got 2.1 gig hard disk
But this one's got 75 zip drives.

I was so hungry for this fantastic, so modern computer,
The nearest my sister's got to 'modern technology'
Is the car hooter.
A strange feeling came over me,
Like I was being stung from the inside by a bee.

Timothy Ballantine (12)
Shoeburyness County High School

INGREDIENTS OF MAGIC

The smell of evil fills the air, as a cauldron boils
and trouble flares.
Life is deadly and unfair, witches cast spells
without any care.
A thumb of a child, the bladder of a goat,
The poison of a frog as well as its croak.
Rats and heads of wolves galore,
Ingredients keep coming, more and more.
And if at sunrise the spell's not complete,
It's not all a waste, for the witch gets a
treat . . . *Yum Yum!*

David Bonsall (12)
Shoeburyness County High School

Love

I am lost in a sea of love,
Where am I meant to go.
I'll love him forever and as long as I live,
So please don't ever go.

He is in love with someone else,
But never ever me.
Why oh why does my heart melt,
It isn't meant to be.

He's tall and handsome,
Blonde hair blue eyes,
He is the one I love.
When I see him I go,
Nearly as white as a dove.

I close my eyes at night,
And see him standing there,
Smiling as if everything's all right,
But I know he doesn't really care.

Chloe Haddow (12)
Shoeburyness County High School

Crystals And Colours

I look in the magic crystal glass every morning.
I see beautiful crystals and colours,
Till one day I see an old woman in mourning.
Suddenly the crystals and beautiful colours
Slowly fade away into small black tears,
And since then I've never seen the pretty
Crystals and colours.

Rachel Rose (12)
Shoeburyness County High School

The Beauty Of A Swan

Ripples in the water, the sun's reflection
mother of pearl.
The slender bird approaches, its head
held high and proud.
Her body a winter rose, soft and silky smooth,
Neck a sparkling snowflake,
Eyes of deep sapphire in a winter snow,
Beak a deep shade of burning amber
glistens as she glides.
Gracefully she spreads her wings.
Effortlessly she glides through the
canvas clouds that sit in the sky.
The river now calm, the only sound the
crunching of golden crisp leaves
beneath my feet.

Thomas Penasa (13)
Shoeburyness County High School

Love

As we walk hand in hand
On the golden sand
The moonlight lighting the path
in front.

As we move a bit closer
Our lips touch tight
all smooth and warm.

Arms round me
All snug and tight
All warm as we look out to sea.

Michelle Kinsalla (13)
Shoeburyness County High School

THE HOUSE

See the old creepy house
Suddenly thunder cracks
People are frightened
You see something scary
A person brave
Up he goes
Suddenly a door opens
Nothing to be seen
As empty as can be
Cobwebs in corners
You hear crackling, bubbling
Spilling and screaming
Go up
Don't come down ever again.

Wayne Morris (12)
Shoeburyness County High School

THE WITCH

The witch was walking in the winter cold,
Trying to get to her castle.
She left her brew cooking on the cauldron,
When she got home the brew was boiling over on her magic book.

Later that night, at midnight,
The witch flew on her broom.
She passed every house in the city, even the bride and groom.
Even when she got home, something mysterious happened.
The witch started shrinking,
She shrank really fast.
When people heard about it, they said *'At last.'*

Nick Brooker (12)
Shoeburyness County High School

THE WITCHES' BAD DAY

In the dark of the night
the witches woke up with a fright
the children had all got loose.
The witches got their broomsticks
and went out in the dark of the night
hoping to find the children
that had got free that night.
Suddenly they were spotted
and dived into a bush
but there was no way of escaping
when the witches finally caught them.

They were taken back to the tower
where the witches turned them to cats
but the spell had not worked
and the cats bit the witches
and they fell into the cauldron
where the witches turned to dust.
All was restored for the children
and they were sent back to home.

Matthew Overall (12)
Shoeburyness County High School

WITCHES

Witches, witches
Beware, beware
They're bound to curse a spell upon you
The swish of a wand,
The chat of a spell,
A frog you will turn
Only tomorrow will tell

The witches are evil
The witches are bad
Shame on them
Where they began
They will end,
And all the evil will begin again.

Natasha Morris (13)
Shoeburyness County High School

THE DARK HOUSE

In the dark house down the street
was a cat on the window ledge,
asleep I think maybe but I didn't know.
Last night I went to see if the cat was dead.
The cat was not dead,
but I was close to having a heart attack.

The house was rotting
and things were falling from the roof,
and there were noises in the house.
I was not going in the house
because it may be a trap,
to lock me in the house with noises that scared me
and I ran away from that scary house.

I wanted to go to that house
but I was not going out tonight,
maybe tomorrow I will see.
I have to go to bed now
so see you in the morning.

Charmaine Breakwell (12)
Shoeburyness County High School

The Rats To Cats

The evil witch was preparing a spell.
Those wretched rats will turn to cats and
I hope I never see them again.

The spell was done and she said
'When they come I'll be ready and they won't
know what's hit them.'

Then they came, she said the spell.
'Those wretched rats will turn to cats and
I'll never see them again.'
They all turned to cats
But I shall keep one, the nicest one to
be my familiar.

Ashley Mills (12)
Shoeburyness County High School

Witches Spellbound

I see her pass
a shadow in the sky
a cough a splutter
and then I hear a
nyeahhhh!

Round and round the cauldron go
in an arm and leg go.

Swirl them round the heat arises
till the meat tenderises.

In an eye and in a toe
round and round the cauldron go.

Katie Brown (12) & Jemma Jarvis (13)
Shoeburyness County High School

ALIENS

I'm fascinated
by what we hear on the TV
That could be them
flying around at night

They probably feel
all slimy and gooey
I wonder
what they look like
probably a ball of slimy slime

They probably come
from the planet Mars
Oh isn't it scary
Oh isn't it scary
Oh yeah
They could be hairy.

Natasha Reed (11)
Shoeburyness County High School

SPELLBOUND

Witches gathered around a bowl,
ready to turn a girl to a mole.
Black cats with bright green eyes
staring into that midnight sky.
Potions banging here and there,
broomsticks flying in the air.
Soon these witches will rule the world
and there will be no little girls.

Nicola Snelling (13)
Shoeburyness County High School

THE DREAM

I love go-karting because it's really fun,
Whizzing round the track as fast as a gun.
The feeling's intense,
Your heart's beating like a drum,
So why not come and have some fun.

I've had many crashes,
But never mind.
I haven't been hurt yet,
But one day I may die.

When I get older I'd like to drive,
On a track or the M25.
I wouldn't mind driving for Ferrari,
But I'll probably just go on safari.

But for now that's just a dream,
It may happen or just be a fantasy.

Ryan Bollu (11)
Shoeburyness County High School

SPELLBOUND

Riding in the night on a broomstick
Pitch black at 12 o'clock at night
Flying over all the houses
Looking to give children a fright.
When she gets back home she sits down and watches the telly
Then she gets some popcorn and fills up all her belly.
Then she hears a child scream and shoots off out the door
She grabs her box of popcorn but there isn't any more.

Daniel Rapley (13)
Shoeburyness County High School

WITCHES

A cackle and a clack,
how about that.
Yes! Witches beware
you never know where.
They're neither here nor there,
witches beware.
What makes a witch?
Is it that gruesome cackle,
or that spotted long nose,
and her big black cat?
Beware of the big whoosh,
at night you might get a fright.
It's probably a witch
roaming around at night.

Carla Boydell (13)
Shoeburyness County High School

WITCHES

On that day called Hallowe'en,
Meet the woman that's usually queen.
She is a witch with her cat Mitch,
She's usually really mean.
She crops up spells, and rings her own bells,
She really is obscene.
With a pointed hat, and spotty nose,
Beady eyes and shaggy clothes.
Don't forget that greasy hair,
She really doesn't seem to care.
So on that Hallowe'en night,
Prepare to get a fright.
And whatever you do *beware!*

Wayne Reed
Shoeburyness County High School

WITCH

As I walk down an alley
I see a dark shadow
I walk closer
I see it is a witch
She looks like an evil witch

As I tap her on the shoulder
She grabs her broom
With a magic spell
She flies in the air
I run closer
Grab her arm
She pulls me
She rips my arm
Then pulls me off

I follow her home
It is on a dark doomy hill
I walk in there she is stirring something
She put my fingers in the spell
Then that was the last thing people saw of me.

Roy Thompson (12)
Shoeburyness County High School

WITCHES

Witches' spells are evil,
Witches' spells are cruel,
Witches' spells are horrible,
Witches sometimes rule.

Witches are dangerous,
Witches sometimes smell,
Witches are revolting,
Witches cast lots of spells.

Witches turn you into toads,
Witches turn you into frogs,
Witches turn you into lizards,
Witches turn you into dogs.

Witches can fly,
Witches can make you cry,
Witches can turn you into a fly,
I wish all witches would die.

Jody Purbrick (13)
Shoeburyness County High School

SPELLBOUND

I am spellbound when I'm hungry,
I can't stop thinking about food.
When I know I can't get some,
It puts me in a mood.
I dream about anything,
Anything that will cure my hunger,
But what will be the quickest,
The quickest thing I wonder.
It could be a Maccy D or Burger King,
I really don't care.
It could be in a round box or square,
I don't care.
Now I've got food,
I'm in a good mood.
It's piled in a mound,
Then I eat it,
Now I'm not spellbound.

Lee Cody (13)
Shoeburyness County High School

REVENGE IS SWEET

Witches.
Pointy noses, with moles,
Clawy fingernails varnished in blood,
Square toes with warts, cuts and moles.

A cat sits on her bony shoulder,
As she trots around the rusty, black cauldron,
With a long wooden stirrer.

Snails slide up her long, bony, green legs,
With bruises, warts, cuts and moles.
Green slime runs down the long stick-like legs,
A long, wooden broomstick lies in the shadowed corner.
She wears a black, dusty cloak,
With curly insects crawling up and down.
Mysterious spells are mumbled,
As she runs around the cauldron.

The cauldron contains skin crawling things,
Ear of bat,
A scent of dog breath and skunk,
Wing of kestrel,
Claw of eagle,
Snake's tongue with acid spittings,
A tablespoon of saliva and her own blood,
And to make the revenge sweet enough,
She bites off three millimetres of her tongue.
Acid spitting, cauldron bubbling,
A strand or two of her hair should finish it off.

Revenge is sweet.

Daniel Allen (12)
Shoeburyness County High School

SILVER OBJECT IN THE SKY

What is that in the sky
Shining brightly in my eye
It looks like it is very high
The silvery shine that comes at night time
That thing is looking at me with its little eyes
This is the thing that makes me so surprised
They are little yellow piercing things
I hate these eyes staring at me
The eyes keep on looking straight at me
This makes everything more scary
As they stare with all their might
Trying to stay up throughout the night
I look back at the object
Squinting so I can see
Now I see a big mouth, blue as can be
I realise there are ears but this cannot be true
As it moves on through the sky
The object is trying to say 'Hi'
I call back and say the same thing
Then I scramble through the bin
In the bin I find what I visualised inside my mind
I scan through the pages looking for something
When I found what I wanted I said 'Why are you here'
Then the object came very near and said 'To find out who you are'
I do not know why it wanted to know who I was
It was probably just some hi-tech trickery
The object got closer and closer until it was at my window
When it was this near I closed my curtains
I saw it still shining brighter than before
I was so scared I ducked onto the floor
When I looked up it was coming through my door
So I just ran as fast as I could down the stairs until all my hairs
were sticking up.

Kevin Rushman (13)
Shoeburyness County High School

I WAS SPELLBOUND

I was alone in the house one night,
All the windows and doors were locked,
It was windy and cold.
I went into the kitchen,
I turned the light on,
It didn't come on,
A power cut!
I heard knocking on the windows and doors,
The telly was flashing on and off,
I huddled up on the furniture.
I heard laughing,
What was going on?
The rest of my family appeared,
All laughing.
They had played a trick on me,
I was spellbound!

Emma Harper (11)
Shoeburyness County High School

SPELLBOUND

Three tired and hungry skaters
Trudging through the snow
Walking past the bare trees
With birds staring down at them and
A bird flying around

An inn sign loose, by the fire
People working, a pile of straw
Leaning against a tree
A blazing fire surrounded
by people working

People joyfully skating on the ice
All the houses covered in snow
And icicles hanging from the roofs
A horse and carriage going slowly past
on the bumpy road

The sea lying motionless
Just below the sky, many trees
Just visible from under the snow
Rocky mountains completely covered
in snow.

Nicola Cook (11)
Shoeburyness County High School

SPELLBOUND

The hunters are devastated
Have given up hope.
As they look around,
They see people enjoying themselves.
Also people struggling to keep warm round a bonfire.
Dying trees and plants
The hunters feel like these trees,
But they don't have anything to look forward to in spring.
They are frozen in the picture forever.
A mill is frozen.
An inn sign battered like the hunters' spirits.
The dogs have to obey their masters, however they wish not to.
They are half-starved to death.
The people on the ice are jolly and cheerful and warm.
When I look at this picture it leaves me silent - spellbound.

Iain McCann (11)
Shoeburyness County High School

THE DANCER

Competitor number 16
Name Leena May.
She walked on and took her position in the centre of the stage.
A few coughs, splutters and a baby's cry,
And then silence as the music began.
What an extraordinary tutu. Emerald green with millions of sequins
Sparkling in the light it was exquisite.
Her ballet shoes were white satin,
With a symbol embroidered on the heel.
Every step was taken with such care and grace,
What serene pirouettes, attitudes, and arabesques,
She flowed across the stage.
Her hands and arms were so delicate,
So tall and slim she is.
She had dark auburn hair swept back into a perfect bun
With white satin roses surrounding it.
The music ended, her position was perfect,
She took a curtsy and carefully tiptoed off the stage.
The audience did not clap or flinch,
They sat with their mouths wide open,
Totally spellbound.

Laura Sage (13)
Shoeburyness County High School

SCARY SPELLS

Scary spells are everywhere,
Scary spells are in the air.
Witches are making scary spells
With dead man's toes and
a dead man's nose,

Witches are making scary spells,
On Hallowe'en night scaring little people,
Till they get a fright.

Witches are snatching little people,
Witches are scaring little people,
The scary spells take long to make,
They take much longer that baking a cake.

Stacey Healy (11)
Shoeburyness County High School

Devils

The devil king shouted out aloud,
'I want you men to do me proud.
You will go to the human lands,
And demolish everything so nothing stands.'
He gave them a gun, a knife, and a sword,
And said 'If you succeed you will get a grand reward.'
They left the planet which they call tower,
Realising they'd arrive within the hour.
When they finally arrived after which seemed like hours,
They realised they'd forgotten their powers.
They couldn't return so they had to go on,
But soon they wished they had gone.
It didn't turn out quite as they planned,
Because the human folk wouldn't give up their land.
The attack went on for many a day,
It finished around about the time of May.
The war was hard and went on for a long time,
The devils had committed a serious crime,
The war went on for over a year,
When it had finished there was a terrific cheer.
It had finally finished on that certain day,
And as for the devils, they all ran away.

Scott Harrington (14)
Shoeburyness County High School

SPELLBOUND

Here I am with my true love,
It feels like heaven,
Like the stars above.
The moonlight will shine upon our hearts,
Until the day we depart.

Hand in hand we hold our love,
His crystal blue eyes,
They're so sparkling and nice,
So dreamy, so bright.

When I'm with him,
My world's no longer dim.
He's the light of my life,
The blood in my veins,
And the beat of my heart.
He's mine,
Forever . . .

Louise Jowett (14)
Shoeburyness County High School

SPELLBOUND

I'm under the spell of love,
When I see him I know I'm in love.
One day I'll make a secret potion,
That will make him fall under my spell,
And he will love me every day,
For the rest of his life.

Nina May (13)
Shoeburyness County High School

SPELLBOUND

Spellbound is a powerful word,
Just like the people who use it,
Witches and goblins,
Fairies and wizards,
to me they're all just a myth.

But there is a more realistic meaning,
The spell of love is more powerful
Than any witch or goblin,
It can put you in a world of your own,
And apart from your partner,
You're there all alone.

Love doesn't come in bottles or potions,
When you're in love.
The world doesn't know, what's going on down below.

David Cartwright (13)
Shoeburyness County High School

DOLPHINS

I love dolphins
They're the best.
I don't think about anything else
Except for dolphins.
I love the way they swim about
Splashing in the sea
Especially baby dolphins they look so cute to me.
You can go shopping mad for dolphin stuff
You can even go and see them.
Wait a minute I've stopped
I'm thinking of something else.
Oh no here I go again.

Sarah Goodfellow (12)
Shoeburyness County High School

SPELLBOUND

They walk in thick snow
Carrying their spears
One dead fox, that's all for supper.
Three birds are watching them, while the other flies.
A fire burns just behind them.
A family keeping warm.
The hounds are worn and tired.

The villagers are enjoying themselves,
On the river's ice.
The waterwheel is frozen stiff, the icicles hang still.
A person carries firewood over the village bridge.
A horse trots through the village, making homes for the birds.

The mountainside, thick with snow,
Sits in silence.
Until Brueghel finishes his painting.
Then all is revealed.

Danny Smith (11)
Shoeburyness County High School

SPIDERS

Spiders spiders everywhere I look,
Spiders spiders even in my book.
They are round and fat,
and big and black.
They are crawling on my hands
and eating all my ham.
Spiders spiders are in my dream,
Spiders spiders their eyes are full of gleam.

Natasha Allen (11)
Shoeburyness County High School

Safe Dream

Middle of nowhere
scarecrows in sight
the moonlight shining over
the long winding path ahead
Where am I now?
I ask as I walk with fear.

Middle of a forest
a small house in sight
dark shadows looming over
a scary unknown kingdom
Where am I now?
I ask as I walk into the house.

Middle of a cauldron
a tall witch in sight
croaking toads jumping over
my body lying in this cauldron
Where am I now?
I ask with scary suspicion.

Middle of my bedroom
my mum and dad in sight
placing the blanket over me
as I lie in the bed
Where am I now?
safe and sound.

Chai-Wai Chung (13)
Shoeburyness County High School

DESTINY

Trapped, trapped inside,
free me free me from it.
Why can't or won't anyone
help free me from it.
It's weird, wild *spellbound . . . !*
I'm trapped for life,
all I have left is me.
Please free me someone anyone
just please free me.
If there really was a God I would
be with my true destiny not just
wasting my time trapped in it.
It is *life . . . !*

Jamie Brown (13)
Shoeburyness County High School

SHOPPING

I love to shop
I drink pop
I like buying clothes, sweets
And different foods
My friends are dudes!
I'd stare at clothes for a while
I would turn into a tile!
When I've finished shopping
I sit and stare
At the things I've bought
Then I would be taught
How to calm down!

Alex Blyth (11)
Shoeburyness County High School

SPELLBOUND

Winter has finally come
to the small town and beyond,
as all people enjoy themselves,
the weary hunters return
with no catch today.

Oh so sad they are
with faces hung in shame,
and the dogs, so bleak,
so thin and tired.
They come home so downhearted.

But across the town they can see
the happy people, skating on the ice.
They look so happy, so cheerful,
even old men having great fun
curling on ice.

The distant town is so bleak
with crisp snowtop roofs
and mountains so tall
with a mist.
It looks so magical.

But if you look closely
you can see everyone frozen
like ice all over,
but this is a time capsule to see.
The return of the hunters so sad to see.

Charlotte Coster (11)
Shoeburyness County High School

TEACHERS

Teachers, teachers are so bossy,
They don't allow you to talk.
They're so bossy they even tell you to sit up straight.
That is too bossy.
Don't you just hate it when they make eye contact.
Doesn't it give you the creeps.
I really hate it when you get caught
with gum in your mouth.
All the say is 'Put it in the bin.'
But isn't it good when you pretend to
put it in the bin but you don't?
I really hate it when you have to stay in for
ten minutes after school.
It's horrific, isn't it?
It is really annoying when the teachers
tell you to stop fiddling.
It's boring, Isn't it?

Mark Pearce (12)
Shoeburyness County High School

SPELLBOUND

Everything is covered
with a white thing called snow.
What is under it?
I do not know.

The hunters are returning
after chasing the fox.
The dogs are cold and muddy
and the hunters are wet through
to their socks!

Mountain tops are covered
gleaming very tall.
Completely white and glittering
waiting for the next snowfall.

Skaters with hats, coats and scarves
on the frozen pond.
Keeping them warm,
is the fire beyond.

Claire Bassett (11)
Shoeburyness County High School

Love

A bright-eyed smile across my face,
For the boy of my dream,
I will always chase.

I cannot even talk,
My tongue is tied
With butterflies fluttering about inside.

He smiles at me,
I fall to the floor.
The love is there,
So do not ignore.

I love him so,
Why can he not see.
Our love together was meant to be.

His hand slips gently into mine.
Lips so sweet and divine.

He has finally noticed I am the one.
The one he has chose out of everyone.

Ella Donoghue (13)
Shoeburyness County High School

SPELLBOUND SPELLINGS

Spelling tests are trouble,
They make your brain boil
And bubble,
Spellings are really weird,
They make you grow a
beard,
Spelling tests last
Different times,
But never get paid a
dime
Even when you put all
Your effort in,
It just gets chucked in the
Bin,
You never win,
You always lose,
But that's just spellings,
Spellings galore

Trevor Hixon (12)
Shoeburyness County High School

SPELLBOUND

Three depressed hunters walking from their kill
With their dogs following and the birds singing above.
They go past five people making a blazing bonfire
Birds chirping in their perches in trees and bushes
A hard-working woman carrying broken twigs in the snow
Five dozen people skating and falling on ice
An old man sitting in the freezing cold snow picking twigs.
In the middle distance there is smoke drifting out of a chimney
A woman dragging a lady across the ice with a rope.

Gemma Doodes (12)
Shoeburyness County High School

SPELLBOUND

In Shakespeare's tale,
A Mid-summer Night's Dream,
A spell full of love was the
mythical theme.

True love is a spell,
That falls upon anyone,
Magically, mystifying,
And full of such fun.

One day that special someone,
Will come strolling along,
And your love for them,
Can never be prolonged.

When a love is so strong,
Its strength gains day to day,
The reality once known,
Soon fades away.

The spell known as love,
Is the strongest human feeling,
Much stronger than anger,
Which erupts when we lose when dealing.

Only one power on Earth,
Can break the fantastical spell,
And that is heartache, and heartbreak,
That rings aloud, like the home time bell.

Samantha Rudd (14)
Shoeburyness County High School

ARGUMENT

I'm drawn to the wall that's next door to theirs,
And I wait for the row to start,
It hypnotises me.

One day he will kill her,
And that's what I fear
He comes home drunk
After drinking a lot of beer.

He starts beating her about,
Oh what can I do?
That lazy drunken lout.

The screaming has started,
The shouting has started too,
Shall I phone the police?
I don't know what to do.

Now it has gone quiet
He's probably gone to bed
and for all I know,
She might be lying there dead!

Jodie Page (12)
Shoeburyness County High School

SPELLBOUND

It is a winter's land
Covered in white,
Three tired hunters come back from no man's land
Staggering home with their fourteen hunting dogs,
Saddened by no kill
Tired and hungry they barely stand.

While down below them,
Red faced skaters skate
On the pond which is frozen.

People are still working on this frozen land,
They are taking twigs for kindling
So they can keep warm from the frozen air.

But far in the distance,
The snow-covered mountains glare
At the owners of the public house
Who are making a burning fire to keep warm,
While the blackbirds stare at the land below,
Like a time capsule stood still.

Gemma Milner (11)
Shoeburyness County High School

WITCHES

In a very dark room
Appeared a big black broom
On the broom appeared a witch
Who gave a horrible twitch
Her pointed nose
Stood like her toes

She's a good cook
With horrible looks
She looks in her book
And finds what to cook

As the witch flies by
She makes the children cry
I wonder why
She made them cry

If you see her in the night
You're in for a fright
So hold on tight.

Stacey Petty-Mayor
Shoeburyness County High School

SPELLBOUND

Bound,
Bound by a love,
A love of a vision,
A vision of purity,
Fresh, clean, precious.

Sunlight,
Bouncing from hill to hill,
Glistening on mountains,
Lost in clouds,
Clouds of refreshing droplets.

Sheep,
Grazing peacefully,
Looks of contentment
Happiness and joy,
Joys of life.

Trees,
Thick and full,
Luscious, exploding with colour,
Spreading on mountains,
Each holding life.

Wales,
A captured view,
A moving view,
I hold in my heart,
Spellbound forever.

Leanne Newman (13)
Shoeburyness County High School

SPELLBOUND

Fourteen tired bedraggled hunting dogs
and three weary hunters,
Return from a hard day's hunt
with nothing to show for it.

Six spindly trees
and a withering bush
covered in snow sit
and watch.

Forty one skaters enjoy
the icy weather
and a dog joins in too
whilst a bird
soars through the sky

A horse and cart carrying hay
trudge on over
the snowy paths
entering a small village.

Snow capped mountains
and a windy river
and many spindly trees
give the impression of a time capsule

Waiting to explode and come
back into life the way that
Brueghel painted it
Four hundred years ago.

Danielle Chelton (11)
Shoeburyness County High School

SPELLBOUND

Pinned to a wall with only the flicker of a candle,
Gunge sliding between her back and the knobbly wall,
Held there by rust ridden iron chains and clamps.

A mysterious figure makes its way through the mist,
Fangs hanging down, blood drip ping fresh from its victim,
Wearing a black, blood stained cloak,
Red face and hands with black menacing eyes ready to kill.

Cauldrons boiling over raging fires,
Bubbling away as the figure drops in a hissing snake,
A red froth forming on top,
With tongues swirling around,
Eyeballs crumbling under the heat.

Jars lined up on a shelf,
Full to the brim with red blood,
Floating particles forming a paste,
Capped with human flesh.

Coming towards me ready to attack,
Venom loaded for the kill,
Mouth open gaping wide,
As the deadly scream of the victim.

Christopher Bysouth (13)
Shoeburyness County High School

EVIL

Cauldrons are black,
As black as night,
Used to mix potions,
Potions of hell.

Werewolves are people under a spell,
Turn into wolves on a full moon
They fly off in the day,
And come back at night to gobble you up.

Black witches are evil,
As black as their cauldron.
Put you under spells,
Spells of evil

Vampires weave spells,
Spells of death.
They like your blood,
Drinking it from your neck.

Blood is red,
As red as fire,
Never washes away,
Always a pool of blood.

Steven Church (13)
Shoeburyness County High School

The Boiling Pot

Into the boiling pot,
everything bubbling,
boiling hot.
Gruesome goblins,
Bats that glare,
Witches on broomsticks,
Zooming everywhere.
Slimy snails that slither along,
Wretched crows that crackle a song.
Little bugs crunch under your feet,
Stick them in, they look good to eat.
A spider's leg, all horrid and hairy,
Something smells, it looks very scary.
Tasty meat from the head of a rat,
Watch it run and then go
Splat!
Into the boiling pot,
Everything bubbling,
boiling hot.

Lauren Moore (13)
Shoeburyness County High School

Love

Love can be as red as a rose,
Some love can be from your head to your toes.
People say love is a bore,
But I bet they've never been in love before.

You could say love is unfair,
Sometimes they don't really care.
Love is sweet, sweet as a dove,
No one can beat the love from above.

Friends and family all over the place,
Putting kisses on your face.
My heart is red blood,
My heart bounces with a terrible thud.

Try try try again,
Love can put you in incredible pain.
Even though people may not have found,
My head will always spin round and round.

Peter Radmall (13)
Shoeburyness County High School

SPELLBOUND

I walked into the playground, with my basketball,
And what I saw, I couldn't believe, it was the best of all,
There it was on the floor,
I went up closer, 'cause I wasn't sure,
I picked it up, held it to the sky,
I was so happy, I began to cry,
I was ecstatic, I couldn't believe it,
There I was holding the winning lottery ticket,
I took it home, checked the numbers,
Four, five, twenty seven, this was wondrous,
Then I checked the rest of them, they matched without a doubt,
I was so happy, exhilarated, I was desperate to cry out,
I stood and there imagined, just what could be,
The two of us, money and me,
A giant house, a swimming pool,
Limousine, I'd have it all,
Credit cards everywhere,
Money here, money there,
As my money began to gleam,
I opened my eyes, damn, it was just a dream.

Kayleigh Hooper (12)
Shoeburyness County High School

SPELLBOUND

It's a cold scene as the depressed hunters return with their dogs behind them.
As they pass the pub where the sign is hanging on one hinge, a family of five is building a fire.
The crisp white snow is lying on the ground and a blackbird is sitting
On one of the tall trees which are covered with snow.
People playing on the frozen pond.
In the distance, birds are flying above the snowcapped mountains.
Two horses were pulling a cart along the icy roads, past the snowy topped houses.
In the distance there were snow topped churches by the icy roads and
the frozen hills are covered with snow.

Joanne Pearl (11)
Shoeburyness County High School

THE WITCH

I was walking in the woods,
I heard a funny noise coming from a bush,
'Who is it?' I shouted. Nobody answered.
Someone laughed.
I got scared and more scared.
Then I started to run,
I saw a lady in the bush as I ran,
'Wait,' she shouted, 'stop!'
Then I froze, I couldn't move.
It was a witch
'Let me go?' I asked
Then she vanished.

Linzi Carrington (11)
Shoeburyness County High School

SPELLBOUND

As the tired, weary hunters come back from the dreary hunt,
The shadowy figures next to the inn watch the men pull the fourteen hungry dogs along with them.
They sit there by the icy inn, so cold and so hungry,
They see the happy children playing on the iced village lake.
There is also a man next to a tree collecting wood for a fire,
The scavenging birds fly overhead looking for anything that's dead,
Two half frozen people are walking over the snow covered bridge next to the motionless water wheel,
Looking only half alive.
In the distance you can see the sea and the beach and the peaks of snow covered mountains.
The reservoir is frozen just like everything else,
All is quiet,
Winter is in full flight.

Robin Gray (11)
Shoeburyness County High School

WIZARD SPELL

It was cold at night,
And it gave me a fright,
No witches about,
Except one dim light.

There was nowhere to go,
But one wizard to show,
who cast a spell on me years ago.

I turned into a cat,
All brown and white,
With a lovely shine of golden light.

Only three years to go,
Till I return to,
The prince that I once was.

Joanne Jowett (11)
Shoeburyness County High School

THE WITCH

There was a witch,
She made you itch.

Her head was bright as peas,
She had a wand that made you
tremble at the knees.

She cast her spells, and awful smells
until one day she fell on the
floor,
and it was clear she was no
more.

Adam Gardner (12)
Shoeburyness County High School

Witches And Wizards

Here's a tale so old and bold,
It is a tale that's never been told,
Witches and wizards fly together,
Always have, over a feather,
Amazed and enchanted,
At their house,
If you look carefully you might see a mouse,
With glasses so bright,
They will give you a fright,
In the dark light,
Of the night,
The witch has gone to look for a spell,
To make your life a living hell.

Kelly Lander (11)
Shoeburyness County High School

Spellbound

Small fingers sizzling away
Purple toes like mouldy maggots
Earwigs crawling up and down
Little slugs sliding around
Loads of worms round and round
Blood of human squelching down
Octopus' legs yellow and brown
Urggle, urggle, goes the stuff
Now it's time to bring it round
Down it goes the witch's mouth.

Katie Bishop (13)
Shoeburyness County High School

SPELLBOUND

The Pegasus is the place of my dreams
Where birds and swans are sure to be seen
But best of all, behind a door
It's full of reptiles and lots, lots more
This is the place I could spend every day
If only it was closer, and not so far away
With lizards and spiders
Monitors and snakes
You name it and claim it, it's yours for a stake
There are books on how to keep them
On housing, food and drink
My favourites are the frogs and bearded
dragons, also snakes can be a treat
Other people say they are slimy
Ugly, crude and vicious too
I don't see why they hate them
They could end up captivating all of you.

Hollie Driscoll (12)
Shoeburyness County High School

MY DRAGON

The dragon was big, smelly,
it had teeth as sharp as razors
and a tail the strength of seventeen rhinos
and had a neck as long as the Dartford Tunnel.
It blew out a fire that went out of its mouth like a bomb
and it hated people who disturbed him while he was asleep
and people tried to kill him
to show they had a lot of courage.

Nicholas Riches (12)
Shoeburyness County High School

The Dying Dragons

Asleep on his bed of gold,
In a cave hiding from the cold,
Remembering the stories told of knights
who were big and bold,
And all the dragons' gold they sold,
As they went into the dragons' fold,
And killed all the dying and old,
The damage the knights caused was untold,
As the dragon population dissolved,
And one last dragon was resolved,
To sleep on his bed of gold
In a cave hiding from the cold.

Adam March (12)
Shoeburyness County High School

Witches

S lippy, slimy, smelly slugs
P igs' hearts as sharp as darts
E verything and anything will take my fancy
L izard legs long and skinny
L ive rabbit's heart and tail
B ulls' eyes to make the tea
O range eyes gleaming in the night
U nicorn feet hard and dry
N ewts' legs long and fat
D ogs' tails skinny and furry.

Lisa Merrin (12)
Shoeburyness County High School

THE WITCH

There she goes zooming through the air
With her long black hat
And her small black cat
On her long thin broomstick
She's as ugly as a pig
With a long fat nose
Her spots as big as tennis balls
Not to speak about her feet
Her long frizzy hair
And her big green eyes
Don't upset her or she'll curse you like a witch.

Warren Franklin (12)
Shoeburyness County High School

CHILDREN'S DOOM

In a far away forest,
On a Hallowe'en night.
Witches are out there,
Looking for a bite.
They find their victim,
Now back to the cottage,
Into the big black pot.
Cooking it hot,
It will feed a lot.
Back on the broom,
Time for the children's doom.

James Dixon (11)
Shoeburyness County High School

Spellbound

You walk in,
There it is,
Right in front of you,
There it is.

The doll's house of your dreams,
The painted house,
The tiny painted flowers,
The windows,
The glass,
The door.

When you open it up you are mesmerised,
The tiny furniture,
The people,
The rooms.
You want to shrink down and live in that house.
You live in a doll's house,
A big one, but a doll's house.

Anna Woods (12)
Shoeburyness County High School

Wizards

Wizard dee wiz,
Wizard dee woz,
A slimy slug that crawls
and glows
A horrible fright
A nasty sight
A lizard with a dreadful bite.

Charlotte Ford (12)
Shoeburyness County High School

SPELLBOUND

As I look through the window,
Of the next shop I pass,
A glimmer, a twinkle.
I turn and glance,
And in front of my eyes,
Like nothing I've seen,
Sit a pair of basketball slamming machines.

They'd give me an edge,
A spring in my step,
Could they make me look better than Shaq?

As I tear up the court,
And with one swift thought,
I'd show I'm the best with my Tom air attack!

But alas I don't have what I desperately need,
So I might as well go back to dreaming,
Of the lay-ups I'd make,
And the slam-dunks I'd take
In my big flashy boots,
I'd be steaming!

Thomas Squires (13)
Shoeburyness County High School

SPELLBOUND

I stood in front of it,
Overpowered by its size,
I couldn't blink,
I was mesmerised.

The cranking and clanking,
As it ticked up the slope,
It got to the top,
All I could do was hope!

My stomach clenched,
My mouth dropped,
I felt sick,
I couldn't watch.

Like nothing I'd ever seen before,
So big and powerful,
I was overawed,
By this fascinating thing.

It came to a halt,
Left me there - speechless,
So I walked away . . .
Spellbound!

Lisa Cousins (12)
Shoeburyness County High School

My Ride On The Nemesis

At Alton Towers my first ride was the Nemesis
I was really excited,
then I read the sign, an hour's wait.

An hour's wait
what am I going to do for an hour?
Talk to my brother
or look at the scenery? What scenery?

Now it's coming to the river of blood
will I cross the river or not?
Maybe I will, maybe I won't,
Now it's up the treasured stairs into the ride.
Will I get scared?

Onto the ride, will I survive?
Take my shoes off
my legs are dangling down
Off we go, too late now.

Scream, scream, scream
and we're away,
round the bends,
up and down,
round and round
then tumbling down
within a flash, it's all over, scared to death
but that's all over.

Now it's time to go and get my photo,
Oh no, it's not my best side
Never mind. Time for the next ride.

Kate Martin (12)
Shoeburyness County High School

Love

Love overpowers everyone,
At different stages of their lives.
Some people fall in love easily and often
Others don't.
You can't fight love,
You love someone forever.
Once you've been caught,
You're spellbound.
You never stop loving once you've fallen in love,
Love can fade, but it can't disappear.

Spellbound!

Suzie Solly (13)
Shoeburyness County High School

Spellbound

Stirring the cauldron
round and round
is this magic
or spellbound
they gather round at night
giving people a big fright,
crooked fingers
crooked toes
crooked eyes
and crooked nose,
do be frightened
do be aware
do be careful
it's a scare.

Charlotte Davis (12)
The Appleton School

I Remember The Night

I remember the night,
I nearly lost my daughter,
My stomach twisted and knotted,
A frozen chill ran down my spine
As I saw her misshapen body
Entering the ward.
The men in white coats,
Appeared from every direction,
Their faces pale and motionless.
There was silence, except for the bleeping of machines,
Hours later, nothing had changed.
A man dressed in white came out,
Then things became clearer.
He told us the car had been speeding,
He tried to brake but the ice was too harsh.
'It took the tyres clean off the road,' he said
Bodies were flung around inside,
Like rag dolls.
That was all we heard of the story,
The man in white was whisked away
I then heard the words, 'She's doing fine.'
The men emerged, relieved expressions on their faces.
From that moment on, things improved
She's now back to the way she used to be,
But I'll never recover.
I'll always remember the night . . .

Angela Faux (15) & Kirsty Paterson (14)
The Appleton School

Shooting Stars

Look at the sky
See what you can find
Sparkling, shining, shooting stars
That leaves us all behind
Where do they go?
I wish I knew
Is it where dreams
All come true?
Do they live or do they die?
As their magic lights up the sky
Where do they go?
I wish I knew.

Jenna Furby (12)
The Appleton School

A Winter's Day

The trees were swaying,
The leaves were rustling.
Everyone was wearing mittens,
Rosy red cheeks and cold faces,
Thick woolly socks, cold chilly feet.
The flames of the fire shooting up high,
Yellow ones, red ones, all mixed together;
Down comes the snow, like cotton wool buds.
Little kids playing on their sledges,
Little faces beyond the hedges.
People laughing and mucking around,
Then the snow stops,
The sun begins to come out.
Everybody is happy.

Samantha Fellows (13)
The Appleton School

SPELLBOUND

I want to write a poem - it's gotta be profound
To tell you what induces me to feel *spellbound*
A Christmas tree sparkling in fairy-tale light
Makes me feel *spellbound* all right.
The sight of a new birth, life newly found,
Makes me feel *spellbound.*
When a face in a crowd jumps out into my heart
It skips a beat, then flutters - it's love - *spellbound* from the start
When I lie on my back on God's earthly ground
I watch the skies in his heavens - I'm *spellbound.*
When I win a tenner on the lottery after gambling a pound
I guess that short euphoria could mean I'm *spellbound*
Spellbound freezes time and motion for a second
It's an unplanned feeling for which you hadn't reckoned
Be it love, magic - or good fortune's final crown -
I get high on that feeling, that hype -
Spellbound!

Hayley Smith (13)
The Appleton School

THE NIGHT OF THE LIVING VIRUS

I remember the night my sister shrieked in fear
as she stumbled to the floor,
The room was filled with a festive atmosphere,
Until a painful silence controlled everyone.

My mother buzzed around the room like an angry bee,
She attempted to manoeuvre my bedraggled sister
into the car.

I waited in the cold, clinical hospital corridor,
Confused and bewildered by the rushing doctors
who were tending to my sister.
My sister endured several hours of pain,
Then the throbbing in her legs subsided.

I remember seeing my sister beginning to walk
Like a newborn foal taking his first steps.
She started uneasy but soon progressed
to a lively state.

Faye Neate, Jo Eggleston, Taryn Diamond & Jane Foley (14)
The Appleton School

Down At The Bottom Of The Garden

Down at the bottom of the garden,
Old rusty lawnmower,
Football once round, now flat and punctured.

Broken toys scattered around,
Tractor once on top, now embedded
deep in the sand.

Big bold shed roof, in desperate need of repair,
Cobwebs stretched corner to corner, edge to edge,
Grass tall and yellow, just like hay.

Raindrops hanging off the leaves of the trees,
Drip, drip, drip as they fall to the ground,
Twigs fallen long and crooked.

Down at the bottom of the garden.

Chloe Farrugia (12)
The Appleton School

THE FOOTBALL MATCH

As the players came on
The cheers became louder.
The whistle was blown!
The cheers went even higher.
It was so amazing.
So many people pushing together,
The little kids
On their dad's shoulders.
Waving their scarves and banners.
As I looked across
All I could see was
A sea of faces
Wearing blue.
Another whistle was blown
A foul! On the red side
The game went on.
The loud cheers came back,
Red! Blue! Red! Blue!
That's all I could see.
That was a close one
So many tries from both sides.
Then I saw
That special goal.
My side!
The red side cheered.
What a roar.
Then somehow,
I knew we were going to win

Emma Reed (12)
The Appleton School

In The School Room

Click, clack, click, clack,
Here comes teacher,
'Quiet everybody, don't make a sound,'
Miss' voice is angry,
She's in an awful mood.
The register is taken,
Names are answered dutifully,
Chairs scraping and pencils rattling,
Everyone getting ready to work.

Click, clack, click, clack,
Miss walks round the room,
Checking we are working,
No one makes a sound,
She settles down at her desk,
Begins to mark some books,
Someone dares to whisper,
So does someone else.
Miss stands up and begins to shout.

Click, clack, click, clack,
She walks around again,
Checking we are working,
No one speaks, no one dares,
She settles down at her desk,
Finishes marking books,
Some look up cautiously,
Checking it is safe,
Someone dares to whisper,
'Come here, you,' Miss says.

Heather Turner (12)
The Appleton School

HERE COMES THE BRIDE

The enormous doors flung open glaring
down at the bride that entered the church.

The organ roared, and the bride walked along
like a cloud floating across the sky.

The mother of the bride crying like a fountain
and the father hugging the mother,
like she was a teddy bear.

The best man looked like a penguin in a top hat,
The groom stalked the bride.

The ceiling had wooden beams
and the floor tiled and shiny
waiting to be stepped on.

The organ stopped and the guests hushed.
The wedding began.

Matthew Guenigault (12)
The Appleton School

SNOW

Soft white fluffy snow falling all around,
It settles thick and comfy like a blanket on the ground.
Cold to the touch, but fun to play,
Snowball fights and snowmen,
But when the sun comes out to shine
It all melts away then.

David Broad (13)
The Appleton School

A Day At The Seaside

Children laughing, playing,
Screams of excitement,
Murmur of people,
Rattling of bags,
A day at the seaside.

Punch and Judy,
Donkey rides,
Playing Frisbee and eating ice-creams,
A day at the seaside.

The blue sea and yellow sand,
Waves splashing and crashing,
Seaweed in your toes and the sun beating down,
A day at the seaside.

Picnics and candyfloss,
Children with fishing rods,
Seagulls squawking and the creaking of deck chairs,
A day at the seaside.

Getting ready to go,
Running to get a last swim,
Children upset getting dressed,
Sad faces on the way to the car,
A day at the seaside.

An empty beach,
All peaceful and dull,
Litter scattered everywhere,
A day at the seaside.

Sophie Lockwood (13)
The Appleton School

MURDER SHE WROTE

Something huddled up on the beach,
Puddles of dark blood,
Clotted on the back of its head
Scalp smashed open.
A slice of white skull showing through.
'He's been murdered!' Ronnie cried
Hands suddenly as cold as death.

Dark uniformed men had formed
a circle around the body.
Such excitement,
He was excited too,
Murder was so exciting, and easy.
Police had scurried to cover the body
with a blanket.

'Well he had to pay,
No more taking fun now,
No troubles no Stuart.'
Buddy opened the door
to face two uniformed men.
Amy watched as he was dragged
into the police car.
'I am sorry Buddy . . . I saw you do it,'
He'll be back she thought,
He always comes back.

Donna Greene (12)
The Appleton School

ATMOSPHERE

Dark, gloomy!
Leaves crackling beneath my feet,
Swaying trees in the wind,
Leaves falling from trees high above,
Ouch!
Who threw that acorn?
Only squirrels in the trees,
Children playing cowboys and Indians
Through the thorny bushes,
Down the hill, 'Mind that tree stump!'
Ssshhhh!
Oh look there's a badger and a rabbit,
Now the place is deserted and so silent,
Children gone home and nobody around,
I want to go home, get out of here,
Where's the way out?
I'm lost.
Everywhere I look looks the same
Help! Help!
Wait, Look! There's a walker's map,
That looks the easiest way out,
I'll take that route,
It's getting dark!
But *phew!*
I'm out of that dark and spooky place!

Marie King (13)
The Appleton School

London High Street

People rushing along the road
Cars whizzing by and by
Tramps sitting in wet damp boxes
All alone with nobody there.

Some people standing in the middle of the pavement
Having conversations
Others are walking along eating and drinking
All dressed smartly for work.

People shouting, cars hooting, all loud and noisy
Waiting at traffic lights
People trying to cross busy roads
Traffic building up.

Jo Shuttlewood (12)
The Appleton School

The Monkey

A monkey was swinging in a big tree
Swinging as happy as happy can be
All of a sudden he grabbed a bad branch
As he fell down the other monkeys laughed
They said 'Why swing in a tree that's rotten
Now you have fallen and hurt your bottom'
The first monkey cried as the others laughed
The monkey said 'Shut up,' went home and grassed
Big Daddy monkey went out and shouted
The small monkeys ran, would have been clouted
The moral of this story this it be
If the wood's rotten don't swing in the tree.

Ashleigh Drake (15)
The Billericay School

A Poem About Our Queen Of Hearts

It's upsetting but true,
It happened so fast,
She'd just found true happiness,
But was it to last?

Hunted by reporters,
And loved by others,
The dazzling royal Princess,
Was always on the front covers.

She helped those who were sick,
And people in need,
By raising their spirits,
No matter what creed.

She fought through it all,
Her bulimia and divorce,
Her life had started to change,
With Dodi as her force.

And through all of this,
She never forgot,
Her two special boys,
Who loved her a lot.

We all miss her smile,
That never did cease,
All we have left to say is,
Diana rest in peace.

Jennifer Hard (12)
The Billericay School

First Sight Of Love!

I caught his eye from across the room,
At the first sight of him my heart went *boom!*
I tried to look away but my eyes were stuck,
I knew then I'd had good luck.

Soon he stood up and walked over to me,
I was so excited and full of glee.
He asked for a rubber - because he'd done his work wrong,
And as I passed one to him, his eyes - they shone.

Later on in the lesson, he called out my name,
I looked up startled, wondering if I'd gone insane.
He'd called me for a reason - I was sure,
But the next thing I knew - he'd walked out the door!

I ran out after him, thinking he'd left me for good,
But our teacher had sent him out - Mr Wood.
It was for calling out in lessons - which we weren't to do,
Everyone did it - even smarty pants Sue!

I knew then - I felt something for him -
Maybe even love,
It was so wonderful, so pretty like a pale white dove.

I'll tell him soon - that's for sure,
But he might find me a huge bore.
No - I've made up my mind - I'll tell right now,
But he might think I'm a 'stupid old cow'!

Oh, here he comes - he's all alone,
I'll tell him before he wanders off home.
'Hey, Craig,' I called and beckoned him over,
'I like you a lot, but so does Clover.'

He just stood there - staring into my eyes,
We kissed, right there, right then, but after we didn't want to say our goodbyes.

Jemma Perry (12)
The Billericay School

. . . Best Striker In The Country?

He arrived with a shower of goals
For three seasons he was top scorer
He captivated hundreds with his skill
And was on the verge of an England place
Then some new signings were made and he lost
His regular place, the flood subsided
Brought on too late in the semifinal
Given no chance the season following
Occupying the subs' bench until the
Final minutes in desperate attempts to
Salvage something from games already lost
He departed London for Manchester,
Leaving Wimbledon richer but poorer
In skill since his departure from the team
He kept us in the Premier League
Can he do the same for Bolton Wand'rers?
Dean Holdsworth, good luck to him at Bolton
But not against Wimbledon I hope now.

Martin Horn (15)
The Billericay School

Is This 'That' Pride?

One foot on the rung to victory or death.
A line of brave-faced boys,
Poised like predators.

The steel sky frames silhouettes of eagles
who toss bombs from their talons.
Then silence.
Deathly hush.
The innocents look at their friends.
Masks of honour and bravery cover the sheer terror of dying.

Heads bowed like religious men.
Prayers muttered to save a thousand souls.
A hopeless situation.
Is this really 'that' pride?
Depression hung in the oppressive air.
A whistle pierced the silence,
Sudden shocks of current shook the line.

They shot up the ladders over fierce, prickly holly
And out onto the misty plain.
Darting through the fire of angry arrows,
Yelling out aggressive threats.
The drained, drooping, drowsy soldiers giving their all.
A second of pride before being thrown to the ground.

Bombs plunging from the heavens,
Landing like the boom of a big bass drum.
Screams range out across the land,
As men were plucked from life itself.
The mud took prisoners to death row,
Where endless limbs and bodies were scattered.

He lay there. His abandoned weapon close by.
One of thousands dead.
Left in suspended animation,
His eyes told of fear and hopelessness.
Wailing winds swept across the desolate battlefield,
Mothers making their desperation known.
The soldier's mud-caked uniform hid his identity.
Another face in the crowd?

Ruth Fallen (15)
The Billericay School

THE CONSPIRATOR

He closed his eyes and took one deep breath,
His mind was filled with fear just like a child's.
Like a cat the hair on the back of his neck was rising,
And cold sweat trickled down his damp face.
He heard others coming and ran in thoughtless fear.
When he turned back he saw nothing but he stayed so
Quiet like a mouse.

He continued on his journey anxious, confused but alert.
He nervously crouched in the shadows,
Waiting for a second, like a lion would his prey,
As the newcomer arrived sly like a fox he called to
Him by name.
When the other saw him he glanced around,
And then he too ducked away into the shadowy night.

From then on till dawn I waited,
But nothing more was there to see.
So I left with one question in my mind,
What conspiracy did they go off to see?

Amy Marshall (13)
The Billericay School

DEATH

Death is nothing
I have only slipped away
to the next room
Out of the light and
into the gloom.

Everyone here in Heaven
is so nice to me
They say you will be here soon
to make me some tea.

I spoke to God last night
and said 'Why am I here?'
'You silly woman' he said
You should have changed gear!

Alex Dorney (14)
The Billericay School

CLOUDS

When I look into the sky
I wonder how the clouds go by?
Is it the wind that makes them flow?
Is it the trees that makes them blow?
Clouds are fluffy white and soft
How I want to show them off
When the sun comes shining through
Then you see the sky so blue
Every day I say a prayer
How I want to end up there.

Katie Wakefield (12)
The Billericay School

Hallowe'en

Hallowe'en is very funny
you go around collecting money

Seeing everyone go round and round
making sure they make no sound

Witches, vampires and ghosts
prowl the night like evil lampposts

But there's a soft side to lampposts
they help you see
but they look like they're looking at me

So this is the end of Hallowe'en
I'm going to be the worst sight you have
ever seen.

Zoie Snazell (12)
The Billericay School

Animal Testing

I feel I am being punished,
For reasons unknown to me.
In silence from fear,
Imprisoned in darkness,
This life is hell.
I long to be free,
Let me go,
Save my soul,
From the cruelty in your mind,
From your neglect,
For I am a flower choking,
Choking in the weeds.

Hannah Warren (14)
The Billericay School

THE PUB

I live in a pub, have done all my life,
My dad ran them all with my mum (his wife),
A pub is a place where you go to meet,
With the friends that you have, then you sit down and eat.
Once we just sold drinks but now we sell food,
We have to keep smiling when the punters are rude.
The staff are happy when the clients don't moan,
As then they earn more tips to pay off student loans.
We don't get a choice on what music to play,
So we get stuck listening to Doris Day.
We've been refurbished so we have more space,
But we're built by a noisy road not a good place.
Sometimes I work in the kitchen and cook the people's dinners,
But I haven't done that for a while, as I've burnt my finger.
People come into my room and turn the music down,
As I turn it up so loud, the bass beat shakes the ground.
I have a dog called Toby but he won't get any thinner,
As people feed him all their chips and then he gets his dinner.
I like to live above a pub as I make many friends,
But all the smoke and customers just drive you round the bend!

William Crighton (15)
The Billericay School

FILLED WITH FIRE

My Nan's cat is filled with fire
He runs and runs and never tires
He jumps about from place to place
The joy of freedom, upon his face

In his garden he is king
This is no place for birds to sing
He stalks and prowls amongst the grass
He runs like a cheetah, so quick and fast

All he wants is love and play
All the time and every day
He brings such joy to her life
With him around she forgets all strife

He moves about like a flickering flame
When he does wrong, he is full of shame
His heart is filled with love and desire
My Nan's cat is filled with fire.

Robert Neale (12)
The Billericay School

THE TEST

You line up outside the room,
The teacher will appear very soon,
Then you file in one by one,
You start to feel very glum.
The paper gets handed out,
'Oh my God,' people shout.
You look at number one,
The teacher says 'Isn't this going to be fun?'
Then she says with a strange grin
'You can begin.'
You wish for a bit of luck,
Then ten minutes later, 'Miss I'm stuck,'
The teacher looks at you with her beady eyes,
'Didn't you revise?'
You hope you don't get done,
'Cos you're still stuck on question one,
Then at the end of the test,
Teacher says, 'You just had to do your best.'

David Green (15)
The Billericay School

The Tiger

Hunted,
Hunted in the bush,
Hunted by a tiger,
He stares at you,
His pussy-cat eyes glare at you.
Hunted, hunted,
Hunted in the bush,
Crouched, poised ready to run,
He glares at you.
Hunted, hunted, hunted,
Hunted in the bush,
His bear-like ears twitch,
He hears you.
Hunted,
Hunted in the bush,
Quick load the gun,
Click!
He hears you.
Hunted, hunted,
Hunted in the bush,
Flat on the ground,
He disappears from view.
Hunted, hunted, hunted,
Hunted in the bush,
The glint of the sun on the lake,
It's too late for you,
Crash! From the water he comes into view.

Joseph Bird (13)
The Billericay School

THIS IS THE LIFE WE LEAD

The wind whistles
over the dry ground.
The town is deserted
Bodies and bones all around.

Many humans are gone
but I remain.
Animals are demented
Things will never be the same.

Leaders said there would be peace
MPs said it would be fine.
But now my family is dead
And I am not far behind.

Every now and again
I see a fellow man.
His legs destroyed by war
Crawling wherever he can.

His arms scarred by guns
His face cut by blades.
His body strapped with bandages
And covered with first aid.

The world has fallen apart
Turned into a kind of hell.
And what disturbs me the most
Is that we brought it on ourselves.

Luke Holloway (15)
The Billericay School

THE WAR

Bullets whizzing around without a sound,
all you see is another soldier hit the ground.
Bombs haunting the spirits of those dead,
but the others have to look at the war ahead.
Walking for days, till they go round the bend,
they have to keep going to the bitter end.
Bones knocking together, like a train on its tracks,
their legs collapse under the weight of their packs.

The cold air penetrating their thin and ragged clothes,
Are their families alright? No one knows.
Their faces twisted with anger and pain,
Will they ever see their families again?
On watch during the day and late at night,
the battle ground looking a bloody sight.
Dead bodies scattered here and there,
like sleeping babies without a care.

They breathe their last breath as they lay down to rest.
Friends have to be strong, it's for the best.
Nothing can be done to keep them alive,
It's every man for himself, they want to survive.
Screams and squeals echoing all around,
as another soldier's been gunned down.
The anguish of families waiting to hear,
Are their loved ones alive? They live in fear.

Nina Gibbons (15)
The Billericay School

The Truth Of The War

As I leave to go to the place I've longed for,
my heart is beating like a big base drum.
The glamorous, glorious, wonderful war,
from where my gleaming, glistening medals will come.

Arrive in the trench, a dug out ditch,
where I am given a grenade and a gun.
I meet the men, like the fabric meets the stitch,
where I am given my durable, drowsy duties to run.

I'm told to go over the top and show no fear,
volcanoes erupting in my face,
a speeding, sharp, streamline spear,
enters a body with no shame and no grace.

I see the soldier dying like a wilting leaf,
bleeding, bruised, black and blue.
I look down on him, pouring with grief,
I'm a helpless child not knowing what to do.

I run along, get on with the fight,
where I see men dropping like flies.
All the glory and glamour is like a dark light,
when I realise the war is just lies.

Fun, fitness, fighting they said,
not chronic, cruel and cold.
No mention of men lying strewn about dead.
The lack of food and warmth we weren't told.

A few years later, when I return,
there's a medal I keep in my drawer.
Not from the fun, fitness and fighting you learn.
No. From the lies and the truth of the war.

Joanne Oakman (15)
The Billericay School

THE CONSPIRATOR

The moon is shrouded in mist.
The darkness engulfs the night.
My stomach is a tight fist.
To keep calm takes all my might.

My long black cloak hides my face.
I stay away from the revealing light.
To be invisible in so much space
Means I can relax ready for the fight.

When I get a guilty pang
I think of Caesar's shortcomings.
Even all the war songs he sang
Can't stop the blood from running.

My heart is thudding like a drum.
I am exhausted and trembling.
While many others are having fun
The conspirators are assembling.

Adrenaline pumps, pressure mounts
As I wait in silent anticipation.
The clock strikes three and Cassius counts.
The magic is beyond imagination.

I finger the blade I will use,
Imagine it smeared with blood.
Conspirators' emotions will fuse
And our anger comes out in a flood.

Laura Cowell (13)
The Billericay School

Poem

My world is a piece of blank paper with specks of dust!
I sit beside my life in confusion,
total confidence sits next to me.

Which? What should I choose?
I feel the breeze against my skin,
but it is not,
it is someone shouting at me,
I have no one to turn to!

The peace has gone in Wonderland.
The world is a piece of paper blank upon my desk.

Gemma Brown (12)
The Billericay School

The Shadow

I sat down in the playground,
and began to eat my lunch.

A shadow fell upon me,
and then I felt the punch.

Then goes the kick then goes the smack,
then goes the names then goes the whack.

Then comes the teacher marching proud,
she struggles to reach me through the crowd.

It's all alright for a day,
and then guess what, they're back to play.

Claire Scoot (13)
The Billericay School

The Storm

From the stillness around, the trees gently move
In the cool silent breeze,
While the garden lays still.
From nowhere, the rain sets in.
Rain, rain, all there is to see is rain.
But then, suddenly from nowhere,
The noise of pitting and patting is quickly broken.
With a flash of lightning and a crack of thunder,
The sky is moved.
Again and again cracks the lightning;
Again and again cracks the lightning and thunder.
It cracks the skies and shakes the air but not
For long before . . .
                                        it begins to retire.
The frightening cracks die away,
Leaving the rain to pitter, patter away.
Now the noise is silenced again and the
Breeze is left to murmur between the trees.
But now the storm has died away,
It will soon return . . . just not today.

Heather Willis (15)
The Billericay School

Bullying

They gather round and start to tease,
And force me down onto my knees.
They laugh and shout and also say,
'We'll kill you if you get away.'

They call me names, that's not enough,
So they start to get rough.
They spit on me, I feel so small,
Then smash my head against a wall.

They get me in the daytime,
also in my dreams,
I can't escape the torture,
That's the way it seems.

On the way to school one day,
The bullying reached its peak.
They pushed me out into the road,
I was off from school for many a week.

Benjamin Chapman (13)
The Billericay School

The Watcher

Feeling sad or feeling sorrow,
What has life got in store tomorrow?
The gentle maiden prepares for bed,
Her delicate mind begins to dread,
Tomorrow - Will I be dead?

Morning comes and she does rise,
Wipes the sleep from her big blue eyes.
Leaving for work, she knows he's there,
Being stalked is not so rare,
Followed - everywhere.

Darkness falls and she heads home,
Begins to fret - she isn't alone.
He's always watching like a hawk,
But hasn't got the nerve to talk.
One victim down, but he'll still stalk.

Debbie Harlow (14)
The Billericay School

BOYS!

Why do all boys insist on being a pain?
They drive us girlies totally insane.
Shouting rude comments when they're with their mates,
And when they're not, they're asking us on dates.
How do they expect us to take them for real?
They never tell us how they really feel.
Should we trust them? - Is it one of their pranks?
I don't think so - thanks a lot, but no thanks.
From one girl to another, they don't care,
I wish they would all learn to brush their hair.
Baggy jeans with no belt is a sad sign,
Wearing scruffy shirts that need a good iron.
Acting hard to become a big bruiser,
Every boy is a total loser.
Using us till the next one comes by,
Then it's 'See you later, sorry, goodbye.'
Why is every boy I know like this?
Is it something out there that they might miss?
All us girls are totally different,
Because the female race is brilliant!

Sheree French (15)
The Billericay School

BULLYING POEM

'Why am I bullied?' a little boy said
I have beatings to my head
I don't go out to have my lunch
Otherwise I get a punch

I kick and scream till someone hears
They pull my hair and scratch my ears
They kick and spit on top of me
They poke my eyes so I can't see

They say nasty things about my mum
They call me names, one is scum!
They get their knives and wreck my clothes
They bruise my ribs and break my nose

I have scars all over my head
Was it just something that I had said?'

Tony Cox (13)
The Billericay School

EVOLUTION

One day a bacteria was born
The next day it spawned
They reproduced day after day
Until the family split and they ran away
They met their love and went to seduce
God what happened? They reproduced
One million years later, they had a girl
She turned out to be a big seashell
A new species was born
You'll never guess what she spawned

The seashell had a child
Fish, amphibians, birds and reptiles
They became different shapes
And there came the ape
After the apes, you'll never believe
Out popped Adam and Eve
Running around Eden, how fun must it have been
They gave birth to Charles Darwin
The discoverer of evolution
Now I come to my conclusion
That we, the humans will live forever.

Jonathan Wong (14)
The Billericay School

WHY I HATE SCHOOL

It starts with the early mornings
Seven o'clock get up
Washing my hair, doing my hair
Putting on make-up just to look fair.

Being at school on time
It isn't very easy
Because it is 8.45
And I still haven't arrived

Registration is worst of all
Listening to Becca, Tess and Vikie
Rabbiting on about homework
That I got an F for;

First second and third lessons
I hate most of all
I'm still asleep
So I doze through them all

Then comes dinner time
The best bit of all
Because I can stuff my face
Till I can't move at all

Then comes last lesson
Oh what a joy
Waiting for the bell to ring
Only an hour till time is mine
(until tomorrow morning).

Jodie Selfe (14)
The Billericay School

DRAGONS

I once knew a dragon
He ate lots of people
He ate a whole house once
Aand our main church steeple.

When I met him
I was in the pub
He walked up to the bar
And ordered a Bud.

After a few beers
We stopped saying cheers
We were talking so fast
Our mouths in high gears.

When we had drunk a few more
The dragon, he was out cold
As he lie there on the floor
He wasn't looking so bold

But just a few days later
He had to fly south
'For winter, you see'
He had said to me.

Four months later
For my friend I waited
When he finally arrived
'I'm back,' he stated.

Phillip Gilbert (15)
The Billericay School

Hard To Say!

Could you imagine being blind?
Would the world be leaving you behind?
Could the world be night all day?
Would you know it's hard to say?

Would your friends like you more
or would they send you out the door?
Could you know what's going on
without knowing, would you last long?

Would you do the things you did?
Would they find you where you hid?
Could you imagine being blind?
You won't know, the world's not that kind!

Karla Sears (15)
The Billericay School

Bullying

He stands above me,
five miles high.
He hits me,
though I don't know why.

Then in the very distance,
the lonely school bell rings.
Then I hear the bully,
laughing at unknown things.

Then as suddenly as he came,
he walked off with his mate.
Now, I am left there crippled,
full of fear and hate.

Laura Walker (13)
The Billericay School

The Rain Cloud

Stealthily floating
through the day,
You better watch out
or you'll be its prey.

The grey sinister beast
which floats high up there,
Every person thinks:
'He is not fair.'

There is a mighty flash
which hits the ground,
and a mighty clap
heard all around.

The pitter-patter on the pavement,
Here comes the rain,
Then a slurping noise
of the combating drain.

There's no stopping it now
as sheets of it fall.
All that can be heard
is the thunder's call.

Then the sun breaks through,
like a brand new day,
sending the rain cloud
on its way.

Ian Yates (14)
The Billericay School

Family Life

My parents are arguing as
my sisters are screaming.
I've got homework to do.
Well that isn't different.

I turn up my music
to blend out the sound.
But then I'm told
to 'Turn it down!'

I don't have much choice
so I do as I'm told.
But how am I to work
with the sound of that uproar?

My sister's in a mood again
Oh how I could hit her!
She's clammed up like a hermit
Why can't she be different!

They're back to square one
and I've got no further.
Then it all goes quiet.
Shall we start over?

Adele Lamb (14)
The Billericay School

Me

Filled with energy,
Cheeky and chatty.
Sporty and speedy,
Noisy and happy,
But also stubborn.

With a craze to shop,
I have addiction,
For clothes, shoes and junk.
Shop until you drop, is my motto
Always in life I run free.

Claire Bedford (12)
The Billericay School

ON THE STREETS OF LONDON

As I lay here day and night,
My life is so full of frights.
All they do is walk on by,
I think they just wish I would die.
I beg for money,
That's all I can do.
They think it's funny, but it could've been you.
All I want is a chance, a chance to live,
Is that too much for you to give?
I used to be someone, I wish I was still,
What if I hadn't taken those pills?
Now my only possessions are the clothes that I wear,
and this cardboard box.
As it gets colder I'll need thicker socks.
My family have gone, I don't know where,
It's obvious that they don't care.
I'm cold and lonely,
No food, friends, or home.
I think I have a few broken bones.
Winter's coming, and I'll still be here.
I have no hope,
Shall I just disappear?

Robert Kerr (14)
The Billericay School

Ten Months

Ten months.
Not enough to say goodbye.
Not enough to leave.
Hold me. I need to know you're there.
I can't see, but I can feel.
You can't imagine.

This is hell.
You're shaking. I sense fear.
Don't be afraid. I'm still here.
Do you still love me?
I feel your tears.
I love you.

I become lost in your arms.
Don't let go. I can't let go.
I breathe you in. I feel safe. I feel warm.
I can feel your heart beating.
My fear subsides. You're still trembling.
This is torture. I hate feeling helpless.

Yet this is what I am.
I don't want to forget.
Ten months. Ten months to feel your tears.
To hear your cries. Ten months is too long.
Lord keep us together. I don't think I could live
Without him.

Nicole Strayer (14)
The Billericay School

ARACHNAPHOBIA

Spiders really scare me.
If I ever see one, I scream, shout, prance about,
and call for mum.
She throws it out the window,
and it runs in through the door.
I think she's drowned it down the drains,
but it climbs in through the mains.
In through holes, up the sink,
it's run across the room, before I've even blinked.
Oh why are spiders so resilient,
all I'm sure of is, that they're far from brilliant.
I really do hate spiders: the creepy crawly things,
I really do hate spiders: the furry frightening things.
Spiders really scare me,
If I ever see one, lurking somewhere,
I just stop and stare,
Waiting for it to skip,
So I can squash it with a stick.
But there's another one, that I don't know about,
secretly spying on me,
While it's waiting for a fly, to become his tea.
It's spun a big web to catch his prey,
but I see him first, and run out of harm's way.
There's a whoops, and a snap.
I've fallen in his sticky trap,
I wonder now what he thinks of me,
I've done to him, what I'd hoped he wouldn't do to me,
but he doesn't react like I would,
he just counts to ten,
and starts again.
Maybe I really don't hate spiders,
they're calm, clever, patient things.

Alison Perry (14)
The Billericay School

A Day Playing Cricket

Padded up and ready to go,
the wicket's been cut,
now let it show.

Blazing sun and lots of fun,
One more run and I'll reach my ton.

All we need are two more wickets,
Yes!
We've got the ninth one,
Keep your nerve,
Bowl one straight,
Put on some swerve,
Oh it swung too late.

Will we do it?
Time's running out.
Come on, we've got a chance,
There's a wicket drought,
Bowled him,
It's all over,
We've won!

Nicholas Butler (14)
The Billericay School

Just Another Day

She wanders the lonely streets, her feet are bare,
Unaware of the staring faces in the world around her.
She wears clothes which are torn and has tangled straggly hair,
Has no family or no home to surround her.

During the day she begs wishing, praying, hoping,
That one day it will be reversed, she will neither be hungry nor cold.
But at the moment her progress is downhill and sloping,
It looks like it will be that way until she's old.

In the evening she walks helplessly back to her park bench,
Newspapers and magazines are her home now.
She hasn't washed for days, she bears an uncanny stench,
As she drifts off to sleep, she's alone now.

So next time you witness this upsetting scene,
Don't just tut and be glad it's not you there.
It's not pity she wants, just the chance to fit in.
We are selfish humans who don't care.

Victoria Jackson (14)
The Billericay School

Have To Buy A Dictionary

I have this problem with spelling see
Which gives me great concern,
It's not that I am thick you know
I'm just a bit upturned.

I try and spell it one way
And then I try another,
I even ask my dad, he says
'Go and ask your mother.'

My mum says 'I don't know,'
This puts me in a spin,
So I end up getting the Tipp-Ex
Or throwing it in the bin.

One day I'll buy a dictionary
And my life will be complete,
And all I'll need to do then
Is make it nice and neat!

Michael Deats (12)
The Billericay School

STARS

Have you ever seen
A shooting star?
I have!
One night last week
Like a giant firework
Streaking through the sky

Have you seen
A pig fly?
He has
Just last month
A giant pig
Big and pink

What's all this?
A UFO
Looks like a disc
Spinning in the air
Sucking up people
For deadly experiments

What's that?
A giant turnip
The size of a house
Big and white
Just right to eat
All succulent and juicy

Oh my God
A small elephant
So small
You could fit it in a spoon
The size of a golf ball
You could put it in your pocket

What the . . .
A tornado
250 miles an hour
Blowing everything over
Houses, trees and lampposts
With a tremendous *bang!*

Ellie Childs (14)
The Billericay School

JUST IMAGINE!

Just imagine if you answered a teacher back,
He'd call you up front, and give you a whack,
With the cane that he held firmly in his hand,
Cheekiness is what Mr Norman couldn't stand.

Just imagine if a food fight broke out,
In the dinner hall, madness would come about.
If all the teachers got covered in potato,
That would be a picture - quick take a photo.

Just imagine if by complete mistake,
A piece of clay landed like a pancake.
Everybody would wait, look and stare,
Until the teacher slipped and landed with her
feet in the air.

Just imagine if the roles had swapped,
And the teachers become children,
Then the discipline would stop!
'Cos if by chance the children became staff,
Then they would definitely have the last laugh!

Sarah Flatman (14)
The Billericay School

Fall Of The Humans

We're killing off our mother Earth,
She who to our race gave birth.
We ruin her oceans and destroy all her land,
Saving the planet too few will demand,
Many of us think that it's bad,
The hole in the ozone layer is sad.
We'll say 'What is this World coming to?'
Then spray CFC smellies all around the loo,
We say that the lumberjacks cutting down trees,
Are the biggest cause of the destruction we see,
But then we throw waste paper into the bin,
Don't bother to take it for recycling,
Look at the traffic, that's the worst by far,
That's what we say as we buy our third car,
Now it's the time for us to change our ways,
Recycle our papers, our thin plastic trays.
Put more people in one car, go to work by bus,
These things we must do to save all of us,
Let's walk, ride or jog to work if we can,
If we want to save the race called human,
And when us humans have died, each and every last one,
This huge lump of rock will still orbit the sun,
New life will emerge, who knows what it could be,
Some thing that can live without an ozone layer, nothing like you or me,
These things could find our bones, buried in the ground,
They'd wonder what killed us, it'd puzzle them how,
A race as large and dominant as we,
Could do something so stupid, so plain to see,
How could we manage to go killing ourselves,
And take the other species down with us as well,
Maybe the bones of us will be ignored,
Or will we make ourselves the new dinosaurs.

Antony Harvey (14)
The Billericay School

THE SCENT OF RESPECT

There's something different about London today,
A certain heaviness I cannot explain.
People weeping everywhere,
Eyes full of tears hearts full of pain.

The air is full of the scent of respect,
Flowers as far as the eye can see.
A mark of sadness for this fair princess,
Whose beauty will never cease to be.

Smiling bravely, two princes walk through the crowd,
A glimmer of tears in their eye.
But alone in their room, in the still of the night,
Two princes ask *'Why?'*

Mari-Clare Speller (12)
The Billericay School

FRIENDSHIP

A friendship is the greatest love of all.
Just think of secrets you share with a friend.
All the problems that you solve together
Just make you think of all the love you share.

Always there to comfort one another.
Makes you feel important no matter what.
If you argue both, it brings you closer.
Even if it started because of you.

I love the way friends never hold a grudge
When you say something out of line that's false.

A friendship is the greatest love of all.
Without my best friend, I could never live.

Katie Jenkins (15)
The Billericay School

MYSELF!

Todd's my name,
and football's my game.
Tottenham's my team,
and England's my dream.

I age at eleven,
and live in heaven (near enough!)
I like cats and dogs,
and hate touching frogs.

I like to have money,
tell jokes that are funny.
I'm a generous man,
with an all over tan.

I always wear clothes,
and then go and pose.
My favourite food's chips,
with nuggets and dips.

I like my CDs,
they tremble my knees.
My most popular track
is Men in Black.

At secondary school,
I'm not such a fool.
It's just like a test,
but I'll do my best.

Todd Row (11)
The Billericay School

TELE ADDICTION

I am a tele addict and people say my eyes are square,
I am a tele addict but I really do not care.
Hollyoaks, Neighbours, Home and Away,
In front of the tele I'll always stay.

BBC 1 and BBC 2 are probably my favourite
channels to view,
But then again there's Channel 4 with ER, Friends
and much, much more.

Three good programmes on in the same time slot,
Which should be videoed and which should not?
Dad's here now to see the football,
I guess I won't see any at all.

Never mind, Mum's calling us for tea,
How I wish for a tele just for me,
But watching X Files alone when it's late,
I think I might get in a bit of a state!

Catherine Cowell (11)
The Billericay School

THE VISITOR

At night my garden comes alive
I know this to be true
The evidence is clear to see
As I'll explain to you

I walk along the path at dark
A rustle I can hear
I point the torch among the shrubs
It's a hedgehog oh so near

It doesn't move as I shine a light
It freezes like a lump of ice
As I go closer
It rolls up like a ball with fright

I move away to give it space
It seems the thing to do
It hesitates then off it goes
Into another space.

Kelly Kendall (14)
The Billericay School

AUTUMN FIRES

In other gardens
And all up the vale
From the autumn bonfires
See the smoke trail

Pleasant summer over
And all those flaming flowers
The red fire blazes
The grey smoke towers

Sing a song of seasons!
Something bright in all!
Flowers in the summer,
Fire in the fall!

Stephanie Gilbert (12)
The Fitzwimarc School

SUMMER ENDS

Summer ends what a shame,
I'm afraid autumn gets the blame,
As the wind blows it's a sign for snow.

Poor old trees,
They have no leaves,
The breeze chills to freeze,
Those poor old leaves.

But what about me I cough and sneeze,
I deserve a nice hot dessert,
But all I get is a cold old bed,
To rest my sleepy head,
Heaters go on fans go off that's how it is from now on.

Mark Warren (12)
The Fitzwimarc School

THE LONELY DUSTMAN

No one likes the dustman,
That lives at twenty-two,
He collects up all the rubbish,
But he never speaks to you.

He walks into your garden,
And drags the bins around,
He empties them and puts them back,
Then leaves without a sound.

He never seems to smile,
Or talk, or laugh or play,
He never gets invited,
And he never seems to stay.

No one ever talks to him,
Unlike our postman, Bob,
He's always fun and happy,
When he's out doing his job.

After the dustman's finished,
He goes straight to his house,
And stays in there all evening,
As quiet as a mouse.

He always looks so lonely,
And I don't think it's fair,
That no one likes the dustman,
No one ever seems to care.

Jenna Kirby (12)
The Fitzwimarc School

THE BEEFBURGER

For two whole days I was locked in the freezer,
Being handled by a grubby geezer.
He put in his hand and pulled me out,
I was crying aloud and started to shout.

He wrapped me up in silver foil,
Then lowered me into boiling oil.
Was this the end? What shall I do?
It looked like the man didn't have a clue.

Twenty whole minutes later,
I felt as hot as the equator.
I was then handled onto a plate,
Was this going to be my painful fate?

I heard the waiter shout and bellow,
To me he seemed like a chubby fellow.
I was put on a table and saw a child,
He added some chilli that smelt quite mild.

He picked me up and licked his lips,
I joined my friends, called the chips.
He swallowed hard and gulped us down,
Hey world, I'll see you around!

Michael Thomas (12)
The Fitzwimarc School

Seven

It starts,
A normal day,
Almost,
I woke up,
I couldn't remember what day it was at first,
Then it hit me,
It was my birthday!
I was happy for a while,
Thinking of all the presents I'd hoped to get,
Then I remembered,
It was the seventh again,
My unlucky number,
Every day since my seventh birthday,
Seven,
My unlucky number.

Andrew Chapman (13)
The Fitzwimarc School

Football Crazy

The sun is like a great big football in the sky,
I wonder how someone kicked it so high.
If I could play professionally I'd be a famous man,
If I could choose a team to play for I'd play for Tottenham.
Every night when I go to bed I have the same old dream.
Glen Hoddle comes to see me play and I am picked for
the national team.
I used to be a normal kid with normal thoughts and hopes
But football's put a spell on me, so all I do is mope.
I wish I could kick as high, as the football in the sky.

Tom Pickering (14)
The Greensward School

Spellbound In Love With Him

Spellbound in love with him.
he makes me warm,
and comfy inside.
Loved by the world.

Spellbound in love with him.
Like a beautiful red rose,
on a bright sunny day,
unable to be harmed by anyone.

Spellbound in love with him.
Hypnotised by his big blue eyes.
I only answer when he speaks,
he's made me spellbound, and happy.

Emma Ashpole (13)
The Greensward School

Casting A Spell

Hubble, bubble, boil and trouble,
Make the spell cause lots of trouble,
On my broomstick far away,
Make my spell work every day.
Turn a handsome boy into a toad,
Ugly, fat, hopping down the road,
Make the boy bumpy and slimy,
Make the boy fat and ugly.
He will no longer speak,
He will only croak,
With the two bloods combined,
We'll wait until it tastes just fine.
Then with crashes of lightning and tons of rain,
The spell will begin and he will never be the same again!

Melanie Rogers (13)
The Greensward School

A WINTER'S NIGHT

An icy chill courses through the crisp night air,
It sends a shiver, like frozen fingers running down my spine.

I stare up at the clear night sky,
At a time like this it is never truly dark.

The moon, a thin, sharp crescent of light,
The grin that was left when the Cheshire cat was gone.

The stars, tiny pinpricks of delicate brightness,
So many patterns to be discovered.

'Orion the hunter', loading his bow.
Cassiopeia, the queen of all she surveys.

I step inside, welcomed by a million blinking Christmas lights,
I clamber upstairs and into my bed.

I go to sleep as soon as my head hits the pillow,
Slowly, I enter a whole world of my own.

Emma Kirby (13)
The Greensward School

SPELLBOUND

Spellbound am I for these things I have seen,
My baby brother when he was born - so small and so clean.
My Nan getting married to a very special man,
The happiness in my family - we are a very close clan.

Spellbound am I for the things I can feel,
My little kitten Jake - so soft and so real.
The sun on my face when I wake up each day,
The buzz that I get from the music I play.

Spellbound am I for the things that I do,
Like dancing and singing - even when I'm blue.
Our holidays together as a family,
All these I treasure in my memory.

Spellbound am I for the sounds that I hear,
The birds that sing - their notes are so clear.
Spellbound am I for all the things above,
How lucky I am to be surrounded by love.

Sarah Toomey (12)
The Greensward School

SPELLBOUND

Sitting there in a haze,
Dreary eyed starting to daze,
Waking up from a trance,
Images before me start to dance.
A loss of concentration,
A total lack of communication,
Looking, staring at a vision,
A sense of confusion.
Swirling patterns all around,
Swaying uneasily upon the ground,
A fixed image is there,
I can't look anywhere,
Other than there.
Such a creation,
Could not be from this nation,
Something so unreal and amazing,
I can't imagine anything,
More entrancing.

Kylie Thompson (13)
The Greensward School

SPELLBOUND

Staring past the world, unconscious of reality,
I see no colour, hear no voice, find no meaning.
My eyes glaze over, while out of the window I lose my focus.
Lost, in the flicker of a flame,
In the break of a wave,
In the smoke of a candle,
I am enthralled . . .

What is important becomes the unknown,
Filling my mind with endless limitations,
Casting no shadow, bearing no resemblance,
Yet hidden in the depths, beneath the surface of confusion,
I find my inspiration,
Compelled by my dream.

Hannah Frost (16)
The Greensward School

SPELLBOUND

S unday morning at 4 o'clock
P rincess Diana died
E ager to see her
L ocals gathered around the scene
L eaning over walls
B uckingham Palace was covered in flowers
O utside the palace people gathered
U nder and over the gates they laid flowers
N othing and no one can replace her
D iana, Princess of Wales.

This is how I describe spellbound.

Emma Souster (12)
The Greensward School

School

Like a line of soldiers,
Marching to the kill,
In bright and shining uniforms,
They walk on still
Spellbound.

Nearer now and nearer,
Closer to the place,
Where they will all
Meet their fate
Spellbound.

Some fight the ranks,
Like a stone amongst the sea,
Until they are in safety,
Pedestrians flee,
Spellbound.

Onwards like the seventh wave,
Rushing ponderously,
Into black old iron gates,
I will them to flee,
Spellbound.

Like a trap the teacher's eyes,
An unabiding hole,
Steely grey, 'your books won't fray',
To stay *obedient* all the day,
Spellbound.

Naomi Bessey (13)
The Greensward School

A Shop Called Spellbound

In a shop far away,
Bright at night,
Dark in day,
A candle glows,
The tarot knows,
What lies deep in everyone.

Glass pebbles,
Smelly sticks,
Different smells,
Full of tricks,
Sun dials,
Wind chimes,
Always changing with the times.

Rebecca De-Koning (14)
The Greensward School

Spellbound

Spellbound,
What does it mean?
The fascination I have seen?
Snowflakes glistening in the sun,
Children having fun, fun, fun.
Tiny hedgehogs crossing the road,
An ant carrying a heavy load.
Miles and miles of thick white snow,
Wow . . .!
My Dad has learnt to sew.
A big snake, really curled,
Spellbound is . . .
The whole wide world.

Claire Cross (12)
The Greensward School

SPELLBOUND

Wandering as if spellbound,
Feel like you're floating around,
What a rush, a flashing light,
Feel like you could dance all night.
Laughing, joking with your mates,
You see everyone with their dates!
The music blasting really loud,
Jumping, singing in a massive crowd,
Suddenly your head starts hurting,
Your mates don't notice, they're too busy flirting,
Reality hits, don't know where you are?
Then you realise you've gone too far,
In hospital you've passed out,
Nurses and doctors are now rushing about,
Drugs aren't worth it, without a doubt.

Laura Wilks (13)
The Greensward School

SPELLBOUND

Beautiful golden sunsets with hints of red and orange shine on me today. As I walk towards the water I see a reflection of the trees waving to me. The birds are high above singing a song with joy. The colourful red blue and pink flowers blowing in the wind. The roaring noise of the wind whistling through my hair. All these things have made me *spellbound.*

Charlotte Frankis (13)
The Greensward School

SPELLBOUND

I want to be a wizard, I want to learn a spell
And if you were a kid, you would as well.
But if I were a wizard, although it would be fun,
I would not find it easy because I am too young.

Ross Gregory (11)
The Greensward School

SPELLBOUND

I am spellbound by what I see,
My eyes transfixed on what is in front of me,
I can't seem to turn away,
I'll remember this for the rest of the day,
And then at night when I'm in bed,
I'll dream of this whilst I rest my head.

Emma Barnard (12)
The Greensward School

SPELLBOUND

Four o'clock, Sunday morning, Paris,
Princess Diana died. People taking pictures
And not worrying about her pain and suffering,
Were looking at her, not caring or calling for help.
Well I was just *spellbound.*

Kerry Waters (12)
The Greensward School

EXPERIMENTS

Do you really think that they
Enjoy the life they lead?
Do you think that you supply
Everything they need?

Don't you think that they might want
A life that's free from pain?
Instead of that they shake with fear
When they see you again.

Do you think you have the right
To use them as you do?
Don't you think that they might feel
Pain, like me and you?

It's necessary, so you say
You play it by the book.
Sit a bunny in the sun
To see if it will cook.

Force a dog to smoke a fag
To prove it harms your health.
Is it fair to hurt them just
So you can increase your wealth?

And half the time you know what your
'Experiments' will do.
I wonder if you'd stop this
If it was happening to you.

Carol Greenland (16)
The King John School

THE GHOST SHIP

Upon the rocks there was a building,
Which cast forth light both far and wide.
This tower seemed to touch the sky,
Red and white went up the side.

The dark night was black and cold,
And as the light went round and round,
There was the glint of a mast,
The keeper thought he heard a sound.

He was curious at the signs,
The keeper peered through the rain.
The man's eyes did not deceive him,
It was a ship and forth it came.

But the man at the wheel was not of flesh and blood,
He was made of nothing but bone.
The rest of the crew were the same.
The 'keeper ran for the 'phone.

It was, of course, the old ghost ship,
And the captain had a cutlass at his hip.
It had gone down with its cargo,
On a voyage, long, long ago.

The ship went forward, not changing its course,
And against the hull the rocks did pound.
Upon the side appeared a massive hole,
And there and then the ship went down.

The crew poured over the sides,
They were going the same way as the boat.
Down they went, into the sea,
The undead, of course, could not float.

And they say, on the right night, through the fog wall,
The ship will appear and once again, meet its downfall.

Keith Smith (13)
The King John School

The Park

Woofing, panting in the park,
We just won't go home till dark,
Squeak, squeak the park swing went,
Rustle, rustle in the hedge,
Children screaming, shouting, talking,
The sound of footsteps, people walking.

Then a whoosh, a tinkle, a ping,
The wind was in the trees again,
Rustling, bustling a hoard of leaves,
Piled up, up to my knees.

The boy with his bubble gum - pop!
The girl sucking her lollipop,
People sat down eating lunch,
Munch,
Munch,
Munch.

Sarah Maddex (11)
The King John School

FREEDOM OF SPEECH

Why do people hide the truth,
Why can't we say what we feel?
Just because someone, won't approve,
Doesn't mean others will feel the same.

From the day we could speak,
We've all had our own views;
And from the day we could talk,
They have been silenced.

The amount of papers, magazines, books;
The amount of silencing.
What's it all for,
But more to the point;
Who's it all for?

Freedom of speech,
Rename it censorship!

Joanne Webb (15)
The King John School

LEAVING

The holiday was drawing near.
I had had a lovely time.
I was in my room packing my bag
Wishing the bag wasn't mine.

I will never forget this lovely place
It was full of fun and things to do.
People dancing and enjoying themselves,
And little children shouting, *boo!*

I will never forget this lovely place
It is going to be quite hard
Going back home to school
And everyone showing me their postcards.

Holly Carder (14)
The King John School

From The Beginning, To The End

I remember the day that we met, the day that this all started.
The day that we first drew close and the day that we parted.

When we first got together, when I first asked you out
I hardly knew you at all, but still I had no doubts.
For what I knew of you, I couldn't have loved more
Your smile, your looks, the person you were,
even the clothes you wore.

I remember our first kiss, the way I felt inside
You made me feel relaxed, loved and cared for,
as if I had nothing to hide.

As time past by, as our love grew
There were no kept secrets between me and you.
For we were so close, we thought we'd never be apart
But you and I were both wrong and left us with broken hearts.

There's not a day that goes by, when I don't think about you
But now it's all over and it's all because of you.

Yet so young, we experienced love
Which took us to the top, to the stars and above.

The hurt I feel inside, I'll never overcome
But the good times overrun the bad and what's been done, is done.

Jo Palmby (14)
The King John School

Badgers In The Woods

In silence I waited,
Breath held hard.
Darkness,
Blindness,
Long gnarled hands extend
Down towards me.
Moon veiled with soft tissue,
Light carved between twisting, winding branches,
Illuminating the peanut butter sandwiches.
One, two
Fat and furry
Three, four
And there's more
Feet padding all in a line
Badgers silhouetted in my garden.

Matthew Gardiner (12)
The King John School

Spellbound

Rotating wildly, trying to escape,
The book was firmly clasped,
In two wizened hands of esteem,
Whilst all the wizards gasped.

And sucking hungrily, flashing white,
Absorbing the air around,
Dragging force into its whirl,
The startled spell was bound.

With ceremonious strength,
The wizard tore the page,
Ripping it into shreds,
And burning it in sage.

The spell had been so evil,
The world was split in half,
No one had ever thought about,
The deadly aftermath.

Alive again and breathing flame,
A rising ferocious hound,
The wizards stopped to stare,
They too were spellbound.

Vanessa Long (13)
The Notley High School

SPELLBOUND

I'm caught in a spell
No way out
It looks like I'm stuck here
In this land of spells.

I'm floating around
Don't know where I am
Surrounded by colours
In this land of spells.

More spells appear
I go and investigate
I start to understand why I'm here
In this land of spells.

Then all of a sudden
I seem to be
Out of the land
Out of the land of spells.

Anthony Overy (11)
The Notley High School

SPELLBOUND

I was a flame,
Flaming in fire,
I was a hare,
Hiding in briar,
I was a drop,
Running in the rain,
I was a scythe,
Slicing the grain.

Axe and tree,
Ship and sea,
Naught that lives,
Is strange to me.

I was a beggar,
Pleading a meal,
I was a warrior,
Sword of steel,
I was a falcon,
Flying high,
I was a deer,
Scampering by.

Axe and tree,
Ship and sea,
Naught that lives,
Is strange to me.

David McLernon (13)
The Notley High School

SLAVERY

Marched to the slave ship
In a great deal of pain
Kept in a wooden cage
For the boat to arrive

Chained down on the boat
Wishing for death to come
Carrying her child
Without a life ahead

Food shoved down my throat
Corpses lying around me
Been sick too many times
Will her baby survive?

Strapped down on deck
Kicking and screaming
Too much pain inside of me
My child has been born

A beautiful baby child
Lying in my arms
No trouble to anyone
Her love, her pride, her joy

The child has been taken
She struggles for it back
Her arm has been broken
Her baby . . . overboard

Fallen ill in a different country
Risk of death is present
Going soon.

Stuart Morley (14)
The Plume School

I Expect I'll Go Next Week As Well

There are many types of people who go on Sunday
there are those particularly good at acting
the vicar included
and there are those like myself who watch.

I watch the actors mostly,
standing proudly with chin slightly raised
in fabrics decorated with flowers or spots
and men in shirt and a tie
as one should be dressed on Sunday.

Then they sing,
there is no tune to their song,
no meaning from the words that leave their lips,
their souls are as flat as the organ
that accompanies their pathetic notes.

It's not just
the people
whom I find
agitating.
It's the whole
pace of the service
the rotating rhythm

and it's the sound
which annoys me
that the yellow service book makes,
as the congregation sound like cattle
when they read the creed.

I've decided that I don't want
to be a robot any longer
and follow the conveyor belt of worship.
I'd prefer to be more passionate and spontaneous
because I don't want the staleness of the church
to affect the bread.

Kate Pratt (16)
The Plume School

Racism

Racism is all around us,
You don't like it but some do.
It's a death row affair,
Sometimes it's funny, it's like a traffic jam,
Always there, going slowly away over time.

It's like rain, different types,
Some thin, some thick,
It's a funny world, I'm aware now.
Don't be surprised if you find hate everywhere,
You learn eventually, you have no choice.

You stated your case time and time again,
You thought about it so what's the matter?
You've lost your place in line again.
It's ironic don't you think?
It's a bloody battle all the time.

You wear yourself out 'cos of this.

Make your mark! Stand up! Shout it out!

Alun Causaker (14)
The Plume School

FREEDOM LOST

I want to be free
I want to get out
To run through the fields
To wander about.

I don't want to be under chains
I don't want to be here
I want to say what I want
Without any fear.

I want independence
To catch the bus
Without segregation
Without any fuss.

Helen Tarling (14)
The Plume School

FEAR

Cautious step,
Pounding heart,
Trouble round every corner,
What have I done,
To make them mad?
Am I really that bad?
Home's in sight,
Almost there,
Out of harm's way.
What was that noise?
Who are they?
Will I die today?

Katharine Youle (14)
The Plume School

Freeze-Frames Of Death

War, horror, what does it all mean?
Blood-chilling photos of death scenes.
Why do we do this to our own kind?
Who could have such a twisted evil mind
As to start the suffering times of terror?

A burnt driver trying to survive,
Will we ever know what he felt inside?
We can only guess and wonder why,
Someone would deliberately want him to die
For money? Oil?

Firework death displays show their power,
But beneath those targets, real people cower.
Waiting for the bombs overhead to pass
Wondering, how long the terror will last.
Hoping, praying that they will survive.

What is all this for?
Sending husbands and sons to war,
This is what comes from civilisation,
War brings devastation, obliteration
Wiping out whole generations.

We should learn from the past
Living in the hope that peace will last,
So that we never again have to see the fear,
Pray for survival and weep that tear,
Freeze-frames of death, the cameras watch.

Hannah Nobbs (13)
The Plume School

The First Day At School

Everyone remembers it,
I remember it.
It was different for me,
I felt different,
I wasn't scared,
At first . . .
It soon became too much.
There were shouts and screams.
At me?
What had I done?
I thought colour didn't matter,
Not any more.
I was wrong.
It had become too much,
I'd let them get to me,
The best day of my life,
Became
The worst.
Why?

Claire Vincent (14)
The Plume School

Lingering Death

Suspended in jet black skies,
Like a hawk waiting to dive,
The feeling of death,
Prickles the skin,
Of all who venture near.

It's a death which is cruel,
Unjustified and mean,
A slow, suffering death,
Of pain and dread,
Enclosed inside a grey, looming wreck.

The iron hulk,
Like a shadow of death,
Drifts on the ebbing tide,
The floating grave of many a man,
Is enveloped in the clouds of war.

The seas light up,
The ship is alive,
With untameable power and heat,
Suffering is hidden behind the curtain of flame,
Of the single, insignificant lives.

John Randall (14)
The Plume School

Poem Of A Slave Ship

I watch my baby being taken away by the white men
Oh please God when will I see her again.

They had me and chain me down to my bed
They leave me alone on my own and unfed.

The white men whip and beat me till I'm black and I'm blue
This can't be happening this can't be true.

Up on deck the water all around
I can't see my baby, she can't be found.

Then suddenly a noise, a sound, a cry
My child, I've got to save her I can only but try.

I run to retrieve her but this time it's too late
This can only be such a sad thing called fate.

The white men take her and throw her in the sea
Wait for me baby, I'm coming it's me!

Jo Messenger (14)
The Plume School

BLACKS' POEM

Why won't you listen
I've got ideas too.

Is it my religion
or something I do.

I walk down the street,
people see and move.

You're ruining my life
and I don't know why.

Then I look in a mirror
and one thing I see

Makes me realise
why you're looking at me.

I am black, you are white,
that's why you treat me
as if you have all the might.

Matthew White (14)
The Plume School

THE AGONY OF WAR

Silence, a deathlike hush,
Flashes of the missile,
The detonation of a bomb,
Unheard, its presence felt,
The murderous rage of all.

The heat of war,
The pain of the kill,
A young soldier, new in his crisp uniform,
He has you in his sights but he freezes,
Still you shoot him dead.

Friends, aliens, enemies, the camera,
Pain inflicted on all but the film.
A crimson flame,
A blanket of fire,
The scars will never surface.

Unyielding pain, it never stops,
Dying children, oblivious of their killer,
The camera whirrs,
Does it have the right?
What's done is done.

Jamie Lauder (13)
The Plume School

BEDROOM

A mountain of colours explodes at the door
One enormous, luxurious cushion swallows me whole
Gorgeous eyes stare down at me
My favourite shoes thrown on the floor accompanied by the jacket
Which has seen so many things!
This is my secret hideaway, I'm surrounded by the things I love
The things that show me - my personality, my true self
I escape from the world and feel safe, secure
To sit alone and think
This place hears my thoughts, shares my secrets, knows my problems
It's always here for me
I can see my closest friends at a reassuring glance
Tigger and Co look at me - how many times they have
Brought me comfort
I get to see the sunrise and the sunset
The wall catches it, my room is created again
I look into the mirror - it's another world, but still it seems the same
This is all mine - my room is my life and my life is my room.

Denise Long (16)
The Plume School

PUNISHMENT

Frightening pain and intense suffering are words that spring to mind,
When I think of the slaves being brutally whipped from behind,
They did no harm to any other man,
But they didn't care - they didn't give a damn!
They still persisted to whip and kill,
Anyone would've thought that it gave them a thrill.
If you wonder what these words all mean,
Try and listen out for the slaves and their screams,
The white people have a lot of explaining to do,
Why did they do it? What possessed them to?
Oh . . . there wasn't a reason! There was no clue!
For the disturbing behaviour they belonged in a zoo!
There is only one way to react to this lot -
It should basically, simply *stop*.

Lisa Gardiner (15)
The Plume School

SLAVERY

There were so many of us,
I was so scared.
We were all packed together,
and each of us cared.

We travelled around from
coast to coast.
Sometimes the hatches
to the slave decks were closed.

We were sometimes allowed ashore,
but made to dance and sing.
They made us stay fit and healthy,
for the money it would bring.

Sadie Bell (14)
The Plume School

WHAT'S THE PROBLEM?

White, brown, yellow and green,
What do all these mean?
Colour
Why all the staring?
Colour
Same inside, outside too,
Colour
Why beat me black and blue?
Colour
It seems to me so unfair
Why treat these people as
if you don't care?
Colour
This is the only reason people change.
Just to see others in pain.
Colour
Jokes and comments stop
them please, others suffer
from your tease,
Colour
This is the bottom line,
Why take the mickey,
Black or white?

Emma Clarke (14)
The Plume School

FROZEN MOMENTS OF WAR (IN THE VIEW OF A PHOTOGRAPHER)

Travelling through time,
In a world that seems mine,
Not really knowing,
Or really showing,
The truth behind the lies.

From one war to another,
Running from cover to cover,
Taking photographs here and there,
But do I really care,
About the truth behind the wars?

It doesn't really matter to me,
As it could just be
A photograph,
But not real life that goes on,
Behind the truth in the pictures.

All it really is, is the frozen moments of war.

Louise Wheeler (13)
The Plume School

RACISM

R acism is all around us, everywhere we look.
A t sporting events it's at its worst.
C ause for concern it certainly is.
I t shouldn't be taken lightly.
S occer fans are the worst, remember the banana incident?
M illwall tried to kick it out, but it came back again.

Mark Wallis (14)
The Plume School

VEGETARIANISM

'Why don't you eat meat?'
  asked my friend's little sister.
'Because meat comes from animals
  who had lived,' I replied.
'But they are bred to be eaten,
  so, why don't you eat meat?'
Well, if you think about it,
  it's like eating one of your pets!
Pets to you, are similar to
  pigs and cows are to farmers.
You tend them, feed them,
  look after them, make sure they're healthy.
The only difference is, *you*
  eat the farmers' animals.
Just think of people who eat rabbits,
  when you next go to feed your pet.'

Susie Barnfather (16)
The Plume School

WHY ME?

Why is it always me?
Does my colour really bother you?
What's wrong with me?
You yell and scream and call me names
But what have I really done?
Why should I wait and not you?
Why should you get new things
And I get hand-me-downs?
Why is it always me?

Kelly Hancox (15)
The Plume School

Said Too Late

I mean to say so much but never do:
Afraid of feelings deep inside of me
As days go by I attempt to tell you
You were the one that taught me how to be.
Your love, example, truth and light guide me
In every task. Without all this just who
Would I be now? A spirit lost at sea.
My strength may fade, but still I'll cling to you.

I mean this, but the words I speak are cold:
Resentful of the fact that I am told
What I should do. Why can't you just be proud
Of me? Must I stand out among the crowd?
My mixed emotions seem to weigh me down.
All this confusion causes me to frown.

Karen Farrell (17)
The Plume School

Aren't We All Human?

I like my life and who I am.
Why can't white people accept that.
I have feelings, I have a brain,
Surely that makes me human.
So why do they treat me like dirt?
Why do they think I'm so different?
It's only the colour of my skin,
I still have the right to live.

I just want to be treated equally.

Rachel Finch (14)
The Plume School

WAR CRIME!

I hear screams echoing in my ears.
What's the point of war?
I see distant faces,
I can't stand it any more!
There's a look of horror on their faces,
As they run out into the street.
If only we could reach out to them,
And protect them from the heat.
The expressions on their faces,
The fear that's in their eyes.
What on earth must be going through their minds,
Will they live or will they die.
Dead bodies lying in the gutter,
Covered in burns and scars.
The sights are sickening,
But I can't help, I feel I'm behind bars.
Oh they need help,
Oh they need care.
Someone to protect,
Someone to be there.
I hear screams echoing in my ears,
What's the point of war?
I see distraught faces.
I can't stand it anymore!

Kelly Ramsden (13)
The Plume School

WAR

The sea was a silent meandering mass of ripples,
It was too quiet for a monstrous cruiser,
Tension filled the air like static electricity,
Steady waves on which they rode would be their end,
Seconds ticked by like a time bomb.
A sturdy humming and hissing began,
A spark became visible like a flickering candle.
Suddenly the open sky was illuminated,
The explosion of death shook the world and sea,
Flames leapt into the deep grey smoke line,
A blinding glare rose from a dark silhouette.
The glimmering reflection made the water look ablaze,
Fear and panic soared from the silence,
Ripping it apart like a piece of paper,
An unbearable stench of burnt gas.
Piercing screams of the remaining soldiers who are burnt alive,
Bigger detonations tore the night into day,
The sky was being terrorised by flames of hell,
Enemy and sea had possessed the great Antelope.

David Wallis (13)
The Plume School

THE BURNT MAN

Here I am, left alone in the dark,
Among a tangled mess of war,
My car is burning, hot and red,
My leg hurts I'm trapped.

I can't get out I'm burning I'm burning,
I try to move but scream in horrific pain,
My leg is burning, bleeding and hurting.
I'm suffocating, can't breathe too much smoke,
Then suddenly I run through with entire pain.

I scream so long, curling and twining,
I listen to my scream, I'm surprised and stop.
I stop and no pain, I can't, it's pitch black.
But then I'm surrounded with a bright yellow light.

I feel I'm floating and drifting, I feel that I'm in bliss.
Then I'm tired and shut my eyes,
Then nothing, no longer.

Claire Edwards (13)
The Plume School

My Teacher's Magnet

My teacher locked me in a cell
With a magnet that looked like a giant bell.
She said 'If you don't find anything metal
You'll live in there with just a kettle.'
So I pointed the magnet towards a chair,
It was broken and battered but I didn't care.
It came straight for the magnet and stuck right there.
In came a cable along with a table,
That was rusty and dusty and stuck to the chair,
A box of staples jagged and labelled
'These are all Mabel's' glued to the table.
So there I was, my arms felt dead.
My feet were aching and so was my head.
All of a sudden I fell with a clatter
And a shatter right down to the floor.
The magnet gave way like a balloon without air.
My teacher came in oh life isn't fair.
'Well done,' she said, 'you need a treat.'
So she put a box of magnets right down by my feet.

Katie McCambridge (11)
The Plume School

THE BURNT DRIVER
(THE POWER OF PHOTOGRAPHS)

We do not know what hit,
He just died.
The golden, glowing flames, curled
Around the once lithe body.
Now he cannot move,
His hands clutch the melted windscreen.
The wind blows, and a patch of skin,
Peels off, and floats away,
Across the wide, arid desert.
His lips are clenched wide,
In a gape of pain and anguish.
His teeth and gums are charred, black and stained.
His eyeballs are gone,
His nose is a charred lump.
His hair is now an invisible entity.
While his skull fights for view,
Out of a pocket,
That once was his head.
Although his vision is gone,
He looks out, forever.
He looks like a monster, never to be looked at as humanity.
You can see the charred remains,
Of the tendons in his once, strong, muscles.
He looks like burnt paper,
On the autumn bonfire.

War is an amalgamation of fear and rage,
And the gore is testimony,
To man's primal instinct.

James Boutle (13)
The Plume School

Freezing The Pain

Freezing the pain,
Not the memory, but the death.
The killing field where the bodies have lain.
The question, why?

Freezing the pain,
Caught in the act of trying to survive -
The burning, the terror, insane.
The question, how?

Freezing the pain,
Will they live to die?
The last breathing body sighs.
The question, when?

Freezing the pain,
Children's bright eyes gleaming,
Not with excitement, with tears and fear.
The question, who?

Freezing the pain,
Picking over the massacred bodies,
Like vultures, but they're not the killing birds.
The question, what?

Freezing the pain,
A twisted mind,
How many killed today?
No answer.

Freezing the pain,
The photographers are there;
Should they show compassion, or should they show shame?
The shutter clicks, freezing the pain.

Claire Sharp (13)
The Plume School

Two Faces

Pity has no power until you make it seen,
As a symbol of tragedy over the field of battle.
There are two faces of war;
            Death and sadness,
            Happiness and hope.

Only one face shows the truth in war.
Images of people dying, crying, mourning and praying.
Angry and puzzled faces
People discovering faces of horror and faces of hope.

The ultimate power of war is sometimes
Only discovered in death and in pain.
A dark threatening sky is a real symbol,
Of death over the field of battle.

Zöe Allen (13)
The Plume School

My Brother

Although I never met you
I feel as though I know you.
All I've seen is pictures,
And stories told about you.
How much love you gave
And how much love you gained.
My life would change if you were here,
No holidays abroad,
No room of my own,
No memories of childhood outings,
Nothing would be simple.
But I'd sacrifice it all,
Just so I could meet you.

Natalie Hodge (16)
The Plume School

CAPTURING WAR

Silence. Nothing to hear.
Waiting for action.
Bombs going off, I whirl around.
Click, click.
Explosions, sparks fly.
I hear the screams that pierce the darkness.
The ground vibrates beneath me.
Click, click.
Screams, burnt children running towards me,
Horror written on their faces,
A girl, an innocent girl.
Click, click.
Everyone fleeing
Away from that place of death.
Trying to get away from the fire, the smoke.
Click, click.
A burnt-out truck stands before me.
A black face stares at me,
Fear frozen on his face.
Click, click.
The charred body, trying to get away,
Trying to stay alive,
But death stands in his way.
Click, click.

Melanie Newman (13)
The Plume School

THOUGHTS

Colours of the room reflected my thought.

Shining, sharply into my eyes. Blinded me.

Blue things, green things, yellow things talk; yet fought
to create the clearness I wished to see.

A problem that was in the way, subsides.

The redness trickled from the tired mess.

Yet still the layers will not budge. I confess

this bright sphere will never let my guilt hide.

But gradually these colours change to merge
into yet a different expression.

Although I know I must forward surge
past the uncoloured rut of depression,
buried deep inside this reflected thought

- I find it hard to know how it was caught.

Vickie Cumbers (17)
The Plume School

HORSES

Jumping freely in the wind
So silky and shiny,
Friendly and joyful when being ridden.
Gymkanas and dressage where horses win prizes,
Cantering gracefully along the beach, in the burning hot sun.
Colours may vary, brown or black,
Other colours if you're in luck.

Emma Newman (11)
The Plume School

THE OUTSIDER

I am the outsider
That nobody likes.

I am the outsider,
The fat one, the different one.

I am the outsider,
The one nobody cares for.

I am the outsider,
The one with no friends.

I am the outsider,
The weird and strange one.

I am the outsider,
I wish I were dead.

Gemma Boreham (12)
The Plume School

TRAGEDY STRIKES

Sound of children screaming,
People crying, praying, wondering,
Film of black smoke, brushed over the sky,
Is your family dead or alive?
The wondering carries on,
Children run over the battlefield,
Hear the sound of hearts beating,
The tragedy carries on,
Suddenly the world falls silent.

Charlotte Hodge (13)
The Plume School

PARACHUTE JUMP

I'm up amongst the white, fluffy clouds
Waiting for my big moment.
I dread to look down,
I'm too high up,
My ears are instantly popping,
I'm shaking,
My heart is beating,
As loud as a drum,
1 ... 2 ... 3 ... *Jump*,
I've jumped,
I'm floating around up here,
It's not as bad as it looks,
I've just pulled the thin string.
All of a sudden the parachute opened
up like an umbrella,
I can see all around me,
The green large patches of land,
It feels wonderful up here,
It's really relaxing drifting around,
I'm relieved to touch solid land.

Charlotte Corderoy (12)
The Plume School

MEMORIES

There is a place where no one knows,
That only few have seen,
There is no sadness, there are no tears,
I wish that I had been.

But in this place of happiness
The glowing spirits show
The painful torment that they suffer
From the memories they know.

Back in the land of suffering
Your loved ones sit and cry,
Thinking and remembering
Asking questions - 'Why?'

In my life there is a space,
And this pain will never heal,
But in my heart and in my soul,
Your memory I shall feel.

Vicky Pegram (16)
The Plume School

THE SEASONS

Autumn

The wind is blowing
The trees are swinging freely
The leaves have gone away

Winter

Winter is here now
The snow is falling on us
All the birds are gone

Spring

Leaves are on the trees
The flowers are blooming again
The sun is warm again

Summer

School has broken up
Summer has reached its hottest
Time for holidays.

Thomas Ellum (12)
The Plume School

The Candle

A single stick
A final wick
To light the way for passers-by
A flicker of the wind disturbs the gentle
Silent flame
Decreasing in size
As the night draws out
Burning away the candle stays
Still and peaceful.
The fresh morning light appears
The candle's flame
Has turned to tears
Reflecting on the clean,
Cut glass.

Samantha Clarke (12)
The Plume School

Solitude

Whenever the thought of you crosses my mind,
I remember when you were warm and kind.
Then reality slaps me like a frostbitten day,
I remember the day they took you away.
My freedom was lost then never to return,
They stripped me of life and left me to burn.
You returned again several years after,
Gone was the happiness and sound of laughter.
I saw you in a light I never had before,
This is what happens when Daddy goes to war.

Karen Anderton (16)
The Plume School

The Painful Grains Of Time

Why do the grains of time
always seem to fall too fast?
Why does tomorrow turn
so quickly into the past?

Why does the flame of a candle
always die so soon?
Why is it not everlasting
letting too many shadows loom?

Why does it always hurt
when a pain goes deep inside?
Why does it never fade
however much you've cried?

Where is your star that shines
so brightly up above?
Don't let me lose your memory
held in my heart of love.

The memories never fade.
The pain will never go.
The flames will always die.
The time will never slow.

You're always there within me
in everything I do.
I have three words to whisper,
they are simply 'I love you'.

Debbie Mansell (16)
The Plume School

The Row

Your shouts are like thunder
that crash in my head
I lie still and wonder
whilst you wish me dead

The stairs they are creaking
with each step you take
my lips they are speaking
but dismissed by your hate

The door crashes open
your anger flies in
no soft words are spoken
whilst you scream of my sin

The walls they are spinning
my anger turns to fear
this is only the beginning
as I feel every tear

Your words are like lightning
striking my heart.
Your expression is frightening
you tear me apart.
Then everything is calm
we stand still and cry.
You meant me no harm
but I say goodbye.

Sophie Parmenter (16)
The Plume School

THE OUTSIDER

I saw her in the playground,
Being teased about her size.
Fatty and pudding they yelled at her.
Tears fell from her eyes,
As they poked and prodded her bulging stomach.
I saw her run towards a door.
Waddle duck they yelled after her
As she tried to pick up speed.
She burst into the ladies' loos,
Crying softly to herself.
Her tear-stained face was such a state.
Just take a minute to think about
How she felt that day.

Louise Etherton (12)
The Plume School

CAN ANYONE ANSWER?

A grey blanket of doom and destruction
Descends upon the unsuspecting village.
Panic-stricken people race,
Jelly petroleum splattering
Clinging to the backs of helpless children,
Burning flesh.
Horrendous screams of pain
Penetrate the night air
Searching, frightened eyes.
Lost children ask,
'Why us?'
Can anyone answer?

Nicola Lunn (13)
The Plume School

Swinging

We are building our world together,
Kandinsky and I -

A city of shapes,
A home of cones,

Under the stairs,
There lay daggers and horns.

The sound of people walking,
Thump along the road,

I lay here thinking will I grow,
In the morning I look as I show.

Sarah Pithers (13)
The Plume School

Teddy

My teddy called Dozy,
is very, very cosy.
He looks a bit battered,
and a little bit shattered,
because I've had him for many years.

He looks a bit unhappy,
and he wears a big red nappy.
He sits upon my cover,
he's my only lover.

He moves his eyes and mouth,
my Nan got him from down South.

Alys Twinley (11)
The Plume School

My Bed

My warm cosy bed I could sleep in all day, all night.
It looks very grand with its headrest blue,
When I jump into bed I feel very safe,
I wriggle down under my covers where no one can see me hide,
My covers look shiny and silky,
My bed feels bouncy and snug.

Helen Hill (11)
The Plume School

A Seed

So small and minute
How can such a giant tree
Fit inside the seed
A magical miracle
That a blind man cannot see.

Gemma Everitt (12)
The Plume School

Hamster

*H*ow cute
*A*re hamsters
*M*any different colours
*S*oft and furry
*T*errible at keeping tidy
*E*verything about them is loveable
*R*eally they are cute.

Louise Woolnough (12)
The Plume School

At Lunchtime

As I threw a bit of a sarney,
It hit the teacher's head.
He looked as if he was going,
To throw a barny.
'It was her' they all said.
As he walked his moody walk,
He turned to me and said,
'I think we need to talk.'
As we strode out,
(me going all red),
'That sarney you threw looked rather nice,
Next time could I have a slice?'

Emma Bolton (12)
The Plume School

The Dinner Ladies' Scam

Quiet lay in the hall,
There was no noise at all,
For the dinner ladies had taken over
And brought the school to rule.

The teachers sat in the staffroom trembling,
The Head the worst of all.
He just kept on mumbling
About how he got this dreadful school.

The children moved silently
Along the corridor,
For now they had to obey
The deadly dinner ladies' law.

Charlotte Mack (12)
The Plume School

Nasty Utd

Nasty Utd, they're a really horrid bunch.
They're so hard they cook footballs
And eat them for lunch.
Nasty Utd, they're as hard as hell.
Nasty Utd, footballers in a nutshell.

One day Utd had a game.
It was the final of the Cup,
And the Nasties had determined
They were only going up.

They looked up at the stadium
As they began to hound.
The world started to shake
And the stadium fell to the ground.

As the game began a Nasty player
Gave a horrendous twitch,
The opposition were so frightened
That they ran right off the pitch.

So if today you're playing them,
You'd better stay in bed,
'Cause no team wants to play
Dreaded Utd.

Tim Collins (12)
The Plume School

Dreams

Lay at night dreaming
Of what the day will bring
Sports, music, people
Just floating in my own world
I love to lay just dreaming.

Kate Leney (13)
The Plume School

Blob

I am a bit of a
pain, my name's Slushy
I am a bit sloppy, slobbery
and I move like a slug.
I move by slithering. I'm made of
Jelly. I eat things smelly. I'm
going down the sewer Weeeeeee!
Splash! Smelly heaven.

Jason Scadding (12)
The Plume School

Mona Lisa

Is it the eyes that are watching your every move.
Or is it in the lips where a smile is hard to prove.
The hair that falls softly around,
The face that's hiding what's been found.
It is hard to explain that the way they're clasped.
That a pair of hands can cause a gasp.
But Mona Lisa's hands are what has made.
This Leonardo's painting an historical display.

Oliver Whyman (12)
The Plume School

Swinging

We are building our world together
Kandinsky and I -

A city of thoughts from the jazz world
A saxophone we hear floating in the distance
The squeak of the clarinet as well in the distance
The melody wiggles about the room
The tempo gets faster the piano joins in
The deep noise of the brass
The sharp noise of the violin
After all the music together
It fades away one by one until it's just the bass playing.

Rachel Staines (12)
The Plume School

The Boy

Detentions and suspensions every day
She takes his planner off his desk
and takes it right away.

She writes a note on the page
But not a detention at this stage.

She waits for him to shout
and moan, she writes a comment on
its own.

He waits after for his planner
She then tells him to mind his manner.

Kerry Mackenzie (12)
The Plume School

Sunflowers By Van Gogh

One vase full of flowers,
Is one vase full of wonder.
Yellow fellows standing in a vase,
And full of yellow colour.
The puffy flowers,
The petalled flowers,
The wilting flowers too.
And I shall share my flowers,
Just me and you.

One vase of flowers standing
all alone,
No one about,
No one at home,
Just one vase of flowers,
Standing all alone,
And who would have thought,
These flowers would be worth so much.
Just one vase of flowers,
Standing all alone.
And I shall share my flowers,
Just me and you.

Lynette Hurley (12)
The Plume School

Never Ending

The hands are drawing a picture for me
I asked them where's the beginning and where's the end
But they refuse to tell me.
They're taking so long because they keep on moving
But some day hopefully they will finish it.

Andrew Renwick (12)
The Plume School

FLOATING

(Using the painting 'Galconda')

Men floating in thin air
As I walk down the street
Am I dreaming?
I continue to walk
Men wearing bowler hats and suits
Standing still as they float.
I'm dreaming,
Pinch myself,
I'm not dreaming
Trying to get away,
Trying to run
From
The floating men.

Stacie McCabe (12)
The Plume School

THE BARN

The old barn door keeps swinging
And the bell keeps on ringing
The wind is whistling through the trees
And there's a cold breeze
In the barn where no one lives
lays a little nest of bees
they buzz all day
hoping for the wind to go away
When the sun sets down
the bees fall asleep
lying in a big heap.

Laura Moseley (13)
The Plume School

Swinging

We are building our world together
Kandisky and I.

A stranger's silhouette deserted in
a storm.

Planets, sun and the sky

A road with an everlasting end.

A house is found round a sharp
but quiet bend.

Dazzling colours, metallic lights.

Cold, windy pitch black nights.

The mystery goes on and yet
to be found.

Still alone without a sound.

Tania Musolino (12)
The Plume School

Tigger, Tigger

Tigger, Tigger stupid cat
would look silly in a hat,
Jumpers, trousers, socks and shoes
he really doesn't have a clue.

Lee Schofield (13)
The Plume School

SWINGING

We are building our world together,
Kandinsky and I -

A home of circles and squares,
swinging through air.

There's a doorway,
Very strange, no door, no nothing.

The stairs are steep and cracked
With thorns sticking out.

The orange lines bright and beautiful,
running down a stream going this way and that way.

The table's very colourful and pretty,
With shapes floating in the air.

This is the world that Kandinsky and
I live in.

Hayley Yates (12)
The Plume School

SPIDER

Spider, spider in your web up there,
as you sit and watch the flies
spinning your web from day to day
As you sit and calmly wait
watching the flies fall on your plate
Watching with your beady eyes
trying hard to spot the flies
As you find the strength to muster
it's time to escape the feather duster.

Andrew Wright (13)
The Plume School

Lazy Dog

Dogs, what do they do?
All they do is eat and sleep.
Easy to keep.
You try to play with him,
but he just goes back to sleep.
The only time they get up is
when they want something to
eat and drink.
They are a bit predictable,
What do they do, dogs?

Matthew Hailstone (13)
The Plume School

The Parrot

As she sits in her cage,
Staring into the mirror,
Thinking of how beautiful she is,
She tries to control the boys,
By flapping her wings,
Showing off her body of colours.
She tries to be best friends with the girls,
Trying to be their school buddy,
Everyone just laughs at her,
She's not a friend to anybody . . .
She walks on her toes,
Swinging her tail feathers from side to side,
Squawking at the people that don't like her,
Some of the pupils wish they could hunt her down and kill her!

Karen Rose Tumbridge (14)
Valentines High School

AN EXCITING MOMENT

Excited is how I felt when I was going to America.
To me the air smelt so sweet,
That I felt like floating in the sky taking it with me.
Just like in my mind,
Where I saw bright pink and neon yellow,
Swirling around making beautiful patterns.
At the same time I heard people dancing around,
Singing sweet songs.
Which makes me taste sugar melting in my mouth.
It's like there are fireworks shooting in the air,
Making pretty colours.
Excited is how I felt when I was going to America.

Aisha Ali (11)
Valentines High School

THE PIGEON

She looks around the classroom,
Looking at the bad little pigeons,
Who are disrupting her class.
She says to them 'Shut up!'
But no one listens.
In her cage she sits
Waiting for everyone to shut up.
They shut up
She blackmailed them
'Shut up or detention!'
There is silence.
She pecks around the whole nest,
She walks, one leg at a time, pecking.

Laveeza Zafar (13)
Valentines High School

OUCH! MY ARM

On Saturday I went swimming
I did acrobatics in the air,
until,
They got the diving board out,
Uh Oh!
I jumped off the first diving board,
Then went on to the second,
Uh Oh!
I went up, went to the edge,
Uh Oh!
Closed my eyes, took a deep breath and
Jumped!
Uh Ohhhh!
I had stuck my arm out.
Ouch! My arm.

Claire Hamilton (11)
Valentines High School

EXCITEMENT - HAPPY BIRTHDAY

The bright blue sky appears for a new day,
The sun in the sky shines bright,
It's someone's birthday today,
A party for someone special,
The tangy tastes of oranges and lemons
And the delicious smell of barbecue.
A sound of excitement outside across the fields,
Fireworks on display at night,
Touch your presents to feel what's inside,
The party ends with a big 'surprise!'

Mahwish Iftikhar (12)
Valentines High School

Drugs

Drugs are bad
They leave you sad

Swallow the pill
and you'll be ill
also in trouble with paying
the bill.

If you inject
you'll end up a reject.

Don't touch pills
They want to kill

Be a boffin
Don't end up in a coffin

Don't be mugs
Say *No* to drugs.

Lucy Geraghty (12)
Valentines High School

The Hyena

Tries to be funny
by making people laugh at others
The hyena makes threats he cannot do
'Maybe I should take you outside
and give you a bite' he growls
He laughs thinking he's funny
but he's not!
He pads around and gets pleasure out of making
fun of people.
But to others he is nice.

Westley Parasram (14)
Valentines High School

The Bee

Buzzing around the room,
And circling around people's heads,
Making the most annoying noise.

Everyone wishing that it would go away
Someone opens a window,
To let this busy little bee out.

This little annoying bee doesn't seem
to want to leave,
Someone picks up a piece of paper,
Rolls it into a ball to swipe away this
little bee.

Everyone is getting annoyed,
Someone takes a last swipe,
And the bee finally flies through
the window.

Peace at last.

Ria McIntosh-Henry (13)
Valentines High School

When I Went To America

When my mum told me I was
going to America,
I could see the bold sky blue,
I could feel air in my face,
My mouth could taste ice-cream,
I could even see myself in the
aeroplane window,
But then I looked down . . .

Benjamin Clarke (11)
Valentines High School

THE LEAD ELEPHANT

Thumping.
The lead elephant.
Flattening everything,
In its path.
The rumble of big,
Loud footsteps.
Destroying everything,
That isn't perfect.
The elephant that
Orders all the others
In the herd.
The elephant that
Travels, but has
The comforts of home.
While the rest get
On with what they have.
The elephant that makes
An unruly herd of elephants
Into an orderly lot.

Scott Lester (14)
Valentines High School

MY NEW PET

Everything was yellow and pink, because I was happy.
My mouth tastes salty I think . . .
I could imagine something furry, like a cat
I could definitely smell cat food, it must be a cat.
I knew I was in a good mood,
Soon I could choose,
A cat which I'll never lose.

Nadine Chatergon (11)
Valentines High School

The Bully

At first I was in fear
I smelt something blue
Then something hit me.

Suddenly my fists went solid
Solid as if I was touching
A brick wall.

My colour through my eyes
Went black
And I saw nothing.

My throat went dry
My taste buds went dry too.

Then the sound I could hear
Was nothing
Except drums which I
Thought was my heartbeat.

M Ahsan Ali (11)
Valentines High School

Babies

Babies, Oh what a joy, bright colours
Like yellow and oranges,
A sweet taste like honey ice-cream,
Babies smell like a rose they smell
like perfume.
I think babies are soft like silk,
Enjoying everything babies have to
Share is great.

Leanne White (11)
Valentines High School

EXCITEMENT

I got excited when we were going to America,
The colour was orange,
Bright and lively.
The smell was night-time,
We arrived at night.
The taste was Coke,
Fizzy and nice like excitement.
The touch was hard,
The firmness of the ground.
The sound was excited people,
Lots of people getting off the plane.

Asmaa Nadat (12)
Valentines High School

MOVING ON

It's the last day of school.
        The sadness inside me.
It's difficult to take.
        Tears running down my cheeks.
It's time to say goodbye.
        Time to leave all the fun behind.
Moving to a different world.
        Trying to forget all I've done.
My friends and teachers all so sad.
        Trying hard not to cry.
I miss them all.
        I've taken a big step in my
                life.

Aadila Ahmed (11)
Valentines High School

Beware Of Strangers

Mary's Mother said 'Beware of
Strangers'
Her Father said 'There are many
Dangers.'

So one day what did she do,
go and ask a stranger
'Where's the nearest swimming pool?'
The man replies 'I'll show you
where
Hop in the back and I'll take
you there.'
So she hops in the back, the silly
girl
His laugh is creepy and his teeth
shine like pearl.
From that day forward things were
not right, the girl had gone
a-missing what a fright.
No one could find her, what a pain.
The girl had gone a-missing and
was never seen again.

Sarah Everitt (12)
Valentines High School

My Embarrassing Trip To Wales

The day of the hill walk came,
I didn't know what was going to happen.
When I ran down the hill,
My trousers started to fall down.

I started to blush pink,
And smelt sweat everywhere.
The nervous dry taste I was tasting
With the shouting for help in my head
And the handfuls of sweat in my hands.

Nicholas Illman (12)
Valentines High School

THE DISCO FOR THE YEAR 6 PUPILS

The school disco started at 6.00 and ended at
7.30,
I went with my friends,
I walked through the door,
Boys were on one side and girls went to explore,
The girls went to the DJ to ask for a
good song,
It turned out that the song they put on happened to
be the famous one,
Macerena it was called,
Everyone got to the middle of the hall,
They lined up in a line
and they didn't notice the time,
During the disco everyone thought that time
just went by,
and when we had to go we heaved a great
sigh.

Gemma Butler (11)
Valentines High School

The Best Day Of My Life

My baby sister was born.
She was warm.
Just woken up.
Soft smooth skin.
And chubby cheeks
She started to cry.
Mum picked her up.
She was sweet and quiet.

Now she's 7
Now she is noisy
Now she is skinny
Soon she'll be in secondary school,
just like me.

Hafsa Pasta (12)
Valentines High School

The Departed

I felt so sad and angry,
When my relative departed,
My mouth felt dry and bland like course sand,
The air seemed grey and smelled raw,
I could not touch anything,
But the sound was soft and quiet.

Simon Waxkirsh (12)
Valentines High School

The Gorilla

She stands outside watching you line up.
One growl and the class is silent.
She gazes inside your eyes and starts talking
in a different language.
She sets you your work and expects it finished
For when she comes around to glare down.
She hears a whisper,
And glares down at the pupil,
She growls again,
And says '*Your lunch is gone.*'
The pupil is scared of her growl,
And frightened when she sees her face.
And the rest of them just watch
The gorilla silently.

Farzana Patel (13)
Valentines High School

Excitement

When I went I could smell the roses
of excitement.
When I went I could hear the loud
jungle music in my ears,
When I went I could taste the
sour bubble gum which made me jump
in excitement,
When I went I could feel the burn
on my fingertips which had me jumping,
When I went I could see the bright
colours that had excitement in it.

Sheraz Razaq (11)
Valentines High School

Our Assembly

Yellow and orange is excitement on the
day of our assembly.
The smell of perfume was drifting in
the air, as everyone was laughing with
smiles on their faces.
The taste of happiness is chocolate melting
in my mouth.
The sound of birds was children singing
and dancing their hearts out.
The feel of silk is joy and happiness,
just like we were on that special day.

Shama Hussain (11)
Valentines High School

Leavers' Disco

It starts at 6.00 and ends at half-eight.
Let's party at Christchurch I hope I'm not late.
I'm at the hall, they shout out my name.
Let's grab the crew, and dance around the room.
Get your partner, let's do the tango
It's time to have a bite of snack.
Let's munch up the Frisps, or we'll have no crisps.
We start to dance again, and here comes the best song.
It's the Spice Girls so let's party on.
It's almost half-eight, it's time to go
I'll probably see you tomorrow.

Reena Bhudia (11)
Valentines High School

The Piano

Hear the music in the air.
I play the piano with no care.
I hate to practise all day long,
always playing the same old song.

Hear the music in the air.
I play the piano with no care.
'You have to practise an hour a day,
to do your best,' My mum would say.

Hear the music in the air.
I play the piano with no care.
I feel like smashing this thing to bits,
putting it in an unknown ditch.

Hear the music in the air.
I play the piano with no care.
I find myself on auto pilot,
my fingers are now turning violet.

Hear the music in the air.
I play the piano with no care.
It seems the time will never end,
it goes so fast when I've met a friend.

Hear the music in the air.
I play the piano with no care.
It's amazing how ten minutes to go
seems just like an hour or so.

Hear the music in the air.
I play the piano with no care.
And now it all comes to an end,
but by tomorrow it will start again.

Jor'el C N Mitchell (13)
Wanstead High School

LIFE

Life
It can be hard,
It can be easy,
You know that.

Watching your every step,
Thinking of the years to come,
Thinking of the years gone,
Thinking of what has become.

All the troubles of the world,
All comes down to me,
Thinking of the birds and the bees,
The blossoms in the trees.

The storm clouds hanging over me,
Raining,
Hailing,
Over me.

Life,
It can be difficult,
It can be easy,
You know that.

Christopher Waldron (14)
Wanstead High School

LONELINESS

Loneliness is like a book in the corner,
Which hasn't been read,
Like a flower in a pot,
Which hasn't been fed.

To be alone in a house,
Is like a room with no dimension,
A man with no name,
A genius with no invention.

Karla Williams (15)
Wanstead High School

THE DREAM

I sleep peacefully,
eyes closed,
thoughts passing by,
happy thoughts, sad thoughts,
good thoughts, bad thoughts,
An image created in my mind.

A weird thought passes by my eyes,
the picture shows a bridge across a river,
I hold that thought tightly,
the clear river shining brightly,
the hills over the edge slightly,
An image created in my mind.

An admiring view from where I was sitting,
there was no sound,
apart from birds singing,
Swans swimming and making ripples,
after their tails and bluebirds whistling,
a silent thought then the rest,
it was one of the best,
It was an image created in my mind.

Gareshma Bhatia (14)
Wanstead High School

LIFE IS LIKE A MOTORWAY

Life is like a motorway
With constant troubles on the way
But where it will end, who can say?
We just travel day by day.

Making sure we stay in lane,
Hoping none of us go insane
Dealing with every day pain,
Putting on the wipers,
To clear the rain.

Some of us carry heavy loads
Like HGV lorries on the road.
Some go fast,
Some go slow,
But where we end up,
No one knows.

Carly Zucker (13)
Wanstead High School

LOVE HURTS

The roses, the choc'lates, the costly nights out,
The promises which he will never keep.
The words, 'I love you' spring to mind,
In you the feelings run deep.

The time, the date, the night is set,
The things to do are chronic.
The hopes, the fears the wishes made,
Are something quite ironic.

The meal, the venue, the evening fades,
The downhill slalom runs steep.
The talks, the letters, the telegrams sent,
Say, 'Sorry we did not meet.'

The tears, the cries, the sleepless nights,
The man has ruined your life.
The brain, the heart, the life on hold,
Oh love, it cuts like a knife.

Sharon Payne (14)
Wanstead High School

FEELINGS

There's a feeling deep inside of me
a feeling of ecstasy!
It started with a soft tender kiss
Which really did feel like bliss!
At the time I was not sober
Come to think of it,
I wish it wasn't over!

People say there's something there,
the looks, the sighs and the care.
Now I do need to know
the feelings he will show
Will it be love
or just hallucination
I need to know,
Will there be
Complication?

Amy Ward (13)
Wanstead High School

Someone In Your Dreams

My love,
My fair love,
It is time, time to awaken.
The flowers have grown,
and the birds have sung.
You enter into the Garden of Eden.
It becomes your habitat and you start to explore.

My love,
My fair love,
You are the sweetest fruit that arises from
the ground.
There will be a struggle for you.
I will come out victorious,
and take you
The showers over the church tower are no
more.

Omar Ahmed (13)
Wanstead High School

Creation

The brush glides over the canvas
As a river flows over a waterfall,
The paint diverting in all directions
As my brain leaks with inspiration,
The colours dictating the outcome,
And when time has ticked long enough,
There is my masterpiece.

Hatice Boza (15) & Sophia Rehman
Wanstead High School

Prescription

Divert the pain in your heart.
Dismiss the ever-growing lump in your throat.
Deny the throbbing
in the tips of your coarse fingers.
Sift away the burn, churning in your stomach.
Block with your sweaty palms
the sour waterfall streaming
from your remorseful eyes.
Remove all blame from your thoughts
and allow your dismay to emerge.
With one swift decision
reject the idea of hate and attempt to reassemble
the love once discovered.
Or, is it never to be love again?

Rowan Wheeler (14)
Wanstead High School

Ever The Lonely . . .

Sunken to the depths of despair,
Gazing out over fields of doom.
Ever the lonely wandering child,
I drift on a sea of bodies
Past redemption or love,
Past hoping, past caring,
They have given up, as will I.
Like many before me,
I drift on alone, all alone
I shall be there soon,
The time has come.

Harriet Sinclair (14)
Wanstead High School

THE PERFECT PET!

Hamsters,
Hamsters will sleep anywhere.
They will eat every table
And any chair.
They will play the piano
With a glare,
And will always catch you unaware
Hamsters,
Hamsters love to hide,
To try to win your pride,
Under piano,
Up the stairs,
In the attic,
And in your drawers.
One more thing I have to say
Beware they lie in wait
Everywhere!

Natalie Fehily (13)
Wanstead High School

FUTURE AS HISTORY

Can you imagine the future as past?
Most would say *'No,'* but it's happening fast.
The future is what is yet to come.
The past is what has already been done.

The computer was invented in 1947
but will it soon be in technology heaven?
Along with the Beatles' old LPs,
and maybe even the invention of keys.

Modern Technology is changing a lot,
and history as we know it will soon be forgot.
Does anyone know what the future holds?
I'm sure no one does until it unfolds.

Is the future population going to be idle and lazy,
Or will the television drive us all crazy?
Can you imagine the future as past?
You may say *'No,'* but it's happening fast.

Louise Panteli (14)
Wanstead High School

THE LITTLE BABY BOY

His face is soft and gentle,
Two earlobes as cute as can be,
With two little eyes as blue as the sea.
One yawn so sweet for us to see
And a pair of lips so cute for people to see.

When days are light the baby sleeps.
All day long there is no peep.
As night-time falls
The baby calls,
He wants to be fed
Before returning to bed.

The baby is now asleep
Maybe without another peep
Until he wakes again
By the sound of a rattling train.

Laura Davies (13)
Wanstead High School

Snowing

When I look,
when I see,
where are the trees and plants?
Not one flower in sight,
or a frog in the pond,
hipping and hopping.
Where is that rain? There is none in sight,
only a warm winter's day, snowing and bright.
no sun to brighten up the day.
Not a duck on the pond, or a bird in flight.
There is no water, just frozen ice,
snowballs, snowballs
being thrown everywhere.

Sean James (13)
Wanstead High School

England v Italy

England v Italy
Wow! What a thrill
Just thinking about it
Gives me a chill.

England will score first
Hopefully not Italy
With Beckham's cross
Put away neatly.

Shearer out injured
The doc says he's nearly dead
Sheringham and Wright
Have to play instead.

Jamie Hoare (11)
William De Ferrers School

SCHOOL HAUL

On my way to school,
I have to haul,
A great big bag of things
Yet I must not sag
Or lean askew,
For if the PE teacher
Sees me he'll nag,
'20 press-ups at
the double, or you boy,
will be in trouble.'

Philip Hart (12)
William De Ferrers School

THE MATHS LESSON

I just don't get it
It's maths again you see
How can you divide
16 by 33?

Long division, short division,
Adding and taking away.
Numbers going round my head
But why don't any stay?

Multipla, multiplee . . .
. . . My spelling's no better you see.
Times tables, they're worst of all,
If you know the answer - *Tell me!*

Vicki Swallow (11)
William De Ferrers School

A Snowy School Day

I wake up and feel like ice,
I get warm I feel nice,
Mum says come on,
I say hold on!

Just changed cosy and hot,
Got my porridge in the pot,
I'm getting ready for the bus,
Got to rush, don't need no fuss!

I'm on the bus feeling cool,
Now I'm near the school,
We are getting near the school and getting
Oh No! It's covered with snow!

Oliver Swainson (11)
William De Ferrers School

The Poem

My teacher told me to write a poem,
But what could I write?
Should I make it rhyme?
Should it have similes in it?
And what could I write about?
Could I write about the weather?
Cats? Dogs? Pigeons?
I can't really be bothered to write it,
I think I'll tell sir that I couldn't do it.

Alex Westbrook (12)
William De Ferrers School

Football Is The Best

I love football,
Football is the best,
None of the players ever have a rest.

They run about all well and fit,
They only eat a little bit.

When they score they're very happy,
None of them are very flabby,
When they lose they're very sad,
They go and be quite bad.

Adam Boorman (11)
William De Ferrers School

Christmas

*C*hristmas is coming ever so fast,
*H*urrah! We all go shopping,
*R*oller skates, toys and many more besides,
I hope everybody likes the presents I buy them.
*S*ome people shop for hours on end,
*T*ogether we decorate the Christmas tree,
*M*um's in the kitchen making mince pies.
*A*ll of a sudden it starts to snow.
*S*tars are shining, it's Christmas Eve.

Kate Hollingsbee (12)
William De Ferrers School

THE RACE

The race takes place
On a day in May

Millions, billions
Squillions, zillions all waiting for the race.

The race takes place
On a day in May

Cheerleaders cheering
Spectators singing

The race takes place
On a day in May

The race takes place
Very, very soon

Dad's cheering
Mum's screaming

The race took place
On a day in May

Nobody here
Until next year.

Adam Biggs (11)
William De Ferrers School

All About My Three Kittens

*A*ll day long I can't wait to see my
*L*ovely, sweet and cute kittens
*L*ively, playing in the garden.

*A*ll my friends say 'Ah they're so sweet'
*B*oth of them are so tiny but the
*O*ther one is so big
*U*p and down that tree they go
*T*yson has got stuck.

*M*y good old Sunny's helped him
*Y*ep he has come down.

*T*hey have now gone to sleep
*H*ere in the basket
*R*eady to have a dream
*E*very night they do this
*E*yes are shut and snoring.

*K*ind and innocently
*I*n come the cats
*T*hinking what they want for tea
*T*in of cat meat that's
*E*very cat's dream
*N*ow they have finished the big cat comes in
*S*o the little ones quickly scurry up that tree.

Rachel Wright (11)
William De Ferrers School

School

*S*chool is so boring on and on it seems to run,
*C*ollecting dinner money, taking the register, sounds like fun, (not)
*H*appy is Miss Smiley as she helps us write a story,
*O*ver to K block for maths with Mr Mory,
*O*ur horrible grey uniforms are so boring
*L*ittle Miss Small think she looks as bright as the morning.

Helena Gretton (11)
William De Ferrers School

My Pet Dog

*M*y pet dog is called Charlie
*Y*et he always wants to play

*P*lay, play, play he always wants to play
*E*very single day he always wants to play
*T*ill the day he gets tired out (that could never be)

*D*illy, dally all day long
*O*ver the hills and far away
*G*osh I still love him even though he always wants to play.

Laura Gardner (11)
William De Ferrers School

Life To Death, Grandad

Life is like sand in a sieve,
Slowly fading away
Bit by bit
Day by day
The sand fades away.
I didn't realise how much
Sand was left - until today.

Ian Newman (13)
William De Ferrers School